The Right Way the First Time

Teaching Your Dog Kindly and Humanely

The Right Way the First Time
Teaching Your Dog Kindly and Humanely

By Alana Stevenson
Copyright © 2007 by Alana Stevenson

For information, contact: www.K9Kitty.com

Published by Training With A Heart, Ltd.

ISBN: 978-0-9794599-0-0

Cover Photos by Kerri Fenn
Cover Dog Photo: Shelter Dog, Milton Animal League
Book and cover design by Vladimir Stamenkovic

Printed in the United States of America

"After reading *The Right Way the First Time, Teaching Your Dog Kindly and Humanely,* there is no doubt that Ms. Stevenson has an impressive understanding of dog behavior and how we can coexist with them without changing who they are. She explains how positive reinforcement can achieve excellent results without the trauma and fears left behind when an animal is trained by punishment. I highly recommend this book as a replacement to traditional training methods. It is easy reading and clearly states what creates the best results for both you and your dog."
- Chris DeRose, Actor, President and Founder of Last Chance for Animals, Los Angeles, CA

"For too many years, dogs have been unnecessarily trained with harsh and combative methods. *The Right Way the First Time* is straightforward, easily read, and will assist caring dog owners in developing appropriate behavior in a compassionate way and in a fashion that will strengthen the bond between dog and owner."
- Lore I. Haug, DVM, MS, CPDT
  Diplomat of the American College of Veterinary Behaviorists

"The author captures beautifully the essence of positive training, telling us what we know but do not always put in to practice: dogs are sentient beings who are just like us in the sense that they respond better to loving leadership that rewards than to leadership by force."
- Lynn Hoover, MSW, CDBC, author of *The Family in Dog Behavior Consulting,* President & founder, International Association of Animal Behavior Consultants, Inc (IAABC)

"As a veterinarian for the past twenty years, I have seen many good dogs that are poorly behaved because their owners do not understand canine behavior. Positive training is the best method I have seen to teach dog owners how their dogs think, and achieve results without the use of punishment. I am going to make *The Right Way the First Time, Teaching Your Dog Kindly and Humanely,* required reading not only for my staff, but for all my new puppy owners."
- Dr. Ilene H. Segal, DVM, Parkway Veterinary Hospital, Boston Canine Rehabilitation Center

"Alana Stevenson's training methods are right on! I highly endorse *The Right Way the First Time*. One of the main reasons pets are surrendered to animal shelters is because of behavior problems which results in thousands of animals being euthanized needlessly. Many times the owners do not understand that with a little patience, time and training any pet can become a wonderful companion. Kindness, compassion and understanding are always more effective than harsh punishment."

- Meredith Fiel, Founder and Executive Director, Adirondack Save-A-Stray, Corinth, NY

"The complex nuances of comprehensive training are well spelled out in *The Right Way the First Time*. Long gone should be the use of "the heavy hand" as de rigeur in behavior modification. It is well known that animals respond best to positive reinforcement for good behavior, rather than negative reinforcement for "bad" behavior. I highly recommend this book for all people who either have dogs or work with them."

- Dr. Jay Jakubowski, DVM, Village Veterinary Clinic, Brookline, MA

1990 - 2002

This book is dedicated to Dolph, my beloved canine
companion of too few years.

Getting the help of a qualified positive trainer can help readers learn exercises in this book quickly and effectively. Lessons, behavioral consultations, and phone consultations are available from Alana Stevenson. She helps to rectify problems that people may be experiencing with their dogs and cats. Contact information is provided on her web site, www.K9Kitty.com.

Contents

Contents

Chapter Two:
Training Techniques

Chapter Three:
Training Exercises

Contents

Chapter Four:
Other Behaviors

Chapter Five:
Behavior Modification for Fear, Aggression, and Anxiety

Contents

Introduction

This book is intended to give people an understanding of how dogs actually learn and interpret the world around them, at least when it comes to their interactions with us, and to give people the basic principles of teaching dogs kindly and humanely without the use of punishments, reprimands, or leash jerks. I hope that by writing this book, I will help readers to understand dogs better and appreciate them for their "dogginess" and intelligence.

For the sake of convenience and consistency, all dogs are referred to as "he" and all humans are referred to as "she." ☺

Chapter One

Positive Training, and How Dogs Learn and Understand the World Around Them

What Is Positive Training?

Positive training means rewarding dogs for what they do. This can be done in many ways. Play, baby-talk, smoochy-kisses, praise, food, games, toys, running, throwing grass for your dog to catch, swimming, walks, and tug-of-war can all tell your dog that what he is doing is great. Showing your dog that he succeeded in learning the lesson that you were trying to teach, is, in essence, positive training.

Positive training is a way of teaching your dog desired behaviors, redirecting and preventing unwanted behaviors, and encouraging your dog to work with you to achieve the best results in a positive, fun way—without inflicting pain, frightening, bullying, or physically forcing your dog to do what it is that you want. Tools and techniques not used in positive training include choke, pinch, or shock collars; jerking on the leash; squirting a dog with a water bottle; hitting; scruff shaking; kneeing a dog in the chest; slamming a dog to the ground; staring; growling; and yelling. It is so much more enjoyable and refreshing to teach your dog what it is that you want than it is to be angry at your dog for not living up to your expectations.

Why There Is No Need for Punishment

There is really no need for punishment. In my view, animals don't entirely understand it (at least when it comes from humans); become easily inhibited, shy, frightened, or agitated by it; and lose a big dollop of self-esteem when it is inflicted. Besides having negative side effects, such as fearfulness, anxiety, shyness, and inhibition of play and spontaneity, punishment does not give a dog the information he needs to succeed. Punishment does not provide a dog with the knowledge necessary to do what the person who is doing the punishing is seeking. It only confuses the dog and perpetuates more anxiety and trouble.

Another problem with negative training (i.e., using punishments, leash jerks, and reprimands to achieve desired results) is that animals do not learn well under stress. The moment any animal, including a human being, is stressed, the ability to learn decreases. If an animal is truly anxious or frightened, learning ceases. Through positive methods, play, and motivation, you can teach your dog to overcome fear and anxiety and to learn behaviors on cue, in response to requests, such as "Sit," "Leave it," "Drop," "Come," "Lie down," and "Stay," without making him anxious in the process.

Dogs Are Social: They Do Everything Together

Dogs are innately social and communal animals. They live, sleep, eat, play, and hunt together. It is psychologically stressful and abnormal for a dog to be left alone. Even if a dog is not in close proximity to another dog, he will usually remain in view of other dogs or follow them. This is very problematic for dog owners who want their dogs to sleep in a different room, who work long hours, or who have only one dog. It is also why dogs will follow the people they are closest to from room to room (the so-called "Velcro" dogs). It is why, when left alone, many dogs do not want to eat or may panic. It is why dogs want to sleep on the bed with you and why puppies cry when you leave them. Even eating is communal. Your dog wants to eat with you and be close to you. This is why your dog may bring food from the kitchen into the living room and eat it while watching you watch television.

Dogs Experience Life in the Present

Dogs experience life in the present, as do many other animals. They are just "going with the flow," interacting with and reacting to their environment as things happen to them. This does not mean that dogs do not remember the past. Dogs, like other animals, remember past events, people, and places. If they didn't, they wouldn't know where their food bowl was located, who you were when you came home, what the leash meant when you picked it up, or where they left their favorite toy.

We can catch a glimpse of what it is like to live in the moment by considering human toddlers. Toddlers know what is safe versus dangerous, pleasant versus unpleasant. Their frustrations, anguish, hunger, and excitement all take place in the present. They don't think of the consequences of their actions or how past events affect future circumstances. And so it is with your canine companion.

This means a number of things when it comes to how dogs learn and interpret our behaviors. For example, if you are interacting with your dog because of something that happened four hours ago, he will not understand. He may remember what happened a few hours in the past but cannot relate your present behavior to a past event. This is another reason why punishing a dog is not very helpful when training. When you reprimand your dog for doing something in the past, he does not make the connection. He assumes that something is going on in the present that is unfortunate and potentially frightening. Likewise, if you interact with him regarding something that happened four seconds ago, he will most likely correlate your behavior with what is occurring at the present second. This is why in dog training, the success or failure of teaching a dog a concept or behavior is dependent on timing. Sometimes, in order to be effective, you must reinforce a behavior within a half-second. If you are off in your timing by even a few seconds, your dog may be very confused about what it is that you are trying to teach him. As seconds pass, so does his understanding.

Unfortunately, by imagining our dogs as people, we set them up to fail to meet our expectations. We assume that they understand much more than they do. Living in the moment is much easier for us to observe than to conceptualize when teaching dogs. When you positively teach a dog a prompted or cued behavior, you realize quite quickly just how precise your timing has to be for the dog to understand you.

Dogs Are Visual, Not Verbal

Dogs learn visually, at least when it comes to their interactions with humans. It is much easier to teach a dog with hand signals, mannerisms, facial expressions, and body language than it is to teach a dog with verbal instruction. Tone of voice also affects how dogs learn and respond to people. Inflection tends to be very important, and dogs tune into sounds and noises that go up and down (such as a whistle), as opposed to the monotonous sound that we might make when we pronounce words like "come," "stand," or "stop."

Dogs do not discriminate among human words easily. Most of the time, dogs are not paying attention to what we're saying, so when we talk to our dogs and then talk to each other, dogs begin to tune us out. When you think that your dog is tuning you out, you are probably right. This is not because your dog is purposely trying to challenge you or be stubborn; rather, it is often because he is simply focusing on other things and not on verbal language, especially from another species! Of course, dogs can learn certain words and some aspects of what we say, but that long-winded dialogue you are having with your dog is more than likely going right over his head (that is, if you are expecting him to take you literally).

Visual signals are the best way to teach a dog quickly and easily. Dogs are sensitive to your body language, the inflection and tone of your voice, your touch, and your proximity. Focus on enhancing your nonverbal communication skills, and your dog will be happy you did!

Body Language Is Meaningful to Dogs

Body language is very important to dogs. How dogs position themselves in relation to one another has significance. If dogs are being friendly, they usually do not face each other directly. They position themselves parallel

Fig 1. Bessie and Jake walking side by side.
©2007 Lauren MacDonald

Fig 2. Jake and Bessie position themselves perpendicularly to each other.   ©2007 Lauren MacDonald

to each other, or they position themselves so that they are standing, sitting, or lying down at perpendicular angles to each other.

Direct face-to-face contact is very intense and stressful for most dogs. If dogs face one another and stare, a fight may ensue, especially if one dog fails to angle himself. Mock attacks during play, when one dog directly charges or faces another, are just for fun. But if this positioning were not preceded by play gestures, such as paw-raises and play-bows, it would be taken much more seriously.

We approach dogs face on. We pet them reaching directly over their heads. We lean over them and stare at them. When dogs approach people, people rarely angle themselves away from the dogs. If we did, it would be a nice gesture. When we face dogs directly and extend our hands toward dogs to pet their heads, we think we are being friendly, but many dogs get a different impression.

Many dogs become aggressive when people lean over them, pet them directly on the head, or stare at them while putting their faces too close to theirs. These gestures and behaviors are threatening and unnerving to dogs. Some dogs learn to adapt to our body language, but others do not. Many canine behavior problems stemming from fear and aggression diminish when people stop facing dogs and staring at them.

Fig 3. Kneeling next to Jake instead of in front of him.
©2007 Lauren MacDonald

Fig 4. Perpendicular and parallel body language.
©2007 Lauren MacDonald

Dogs Have an Oppositional Reflex

Dogs love tug-of-war because they have an oppositional reflex. When dogs feel a force, a push against or pull on them, they will instinctively push or pull in the opposite direction. Have you noticed that when your dog approaches you and you push him away, he may get more excited and keep pushing himself toward you? Or that the more you pull back on the leash, the more your dog seems to pull against you? When you push your dog down for jumping on you, you are encouraging him to jump back up because he is instinctively going against the force that you exerted. This is why you should not push him away from you when he jumps on you, close his mouth if he is play-biting, or pull back on the leash if he is pulling. By doing so, you may make the problem much worse.

Dogs Do Not Respect Property Rights; Ownership Changes Hands

If an item is in a dog's mouth or under his paws, it is rightfully his. He has possession of the item at that moment. If nobody possesses an object, it is up for grabs. Dogs view ownership very much the same way that human toddlers do. If an item of yours is not in your possession, which means that you are not actively holding, focusing on, or eating the object, it is not your property.

Dogs don't naturally understand property rights. In dog culture, if a dog does not let go of an item or does not walk away from it, it rightfully belongs to that dog. When a dog stops focusing on an object or becomes distracted and walks away from an object, another dog will take possession of it. *Ownership of an object changes according to who has it in the moment.* Normally dogs do not remove items directly from other dogs' mouths. It is rude, improper doggy etiquette. Fights can ensue when it is unclear to whom an item belongs, such as when two dogs approach an object at the same time. This is also why dogs growl at people when people approach items that they love. Dogs are saying, "Back off." It doesn't matter if it is your wallet, your cell phone, your underwear, or your socks. If your dog has it, it's his. It doesn't belong to you anymore.

Dogs Learn by Association

Animals learn by association. Webster's dictionary defines "association" as "a connection in the mind between ideas, sensations, memories, etc." Dogs make connections by pairing events or sensations that occur simultaneously.

Not understanding that dogs learn this way can cause a lot of misunderstandings and can lead to many behavioral problems in our dogs. For instance, if you jerk on the leash every time your dog sees a person, he will think that the next time he sees someone, he will be jerked or yanked. You might think that you are correcting his unwanted behavior, such as jumping, barking, or lunging. Your dog, however, has not made this connection. He may assume that every time a person passes, you will jerk or punish him. Over time, he may establish a negative association with people and become fearful, aggressive, or overly submissive. This can happen when you punish your dog around other dogs, children, motorcyclists, bicyclists, skateboarders, or guests at the door. As a direct result of your frequent reprimands, scolding, and punishments, he is now reacting around these triggers more frequently and with less provocation.

Why contribute more stress or anxiety to an event or situation your dog already feels upset or nervous about? Getting angry at your dog for being upset, anxious, or stressed out is, of course, not the best way to teach him to calm down. You will find that you can change many of your dog's fearful or negative emotions by pairing positive things with things that he dislikes or finds unpleasant.

Dogs Learn in the Environment in Which You Teach Them

Dogs learn according to the context in which you teach them. If you teach your dog a behavior in the kitchen, he will think the behavior is linked to the kitchen. If you always teach him a behavior in the living room and then you assume that he will perform the behavior in the hallway or on the patio when friends are over, he will probably disappoint you. You didn't teach him the behavior in the hallway or on the patio—you always taught him the behavior in the living room!

You have to teach a behavior in the environment in which you want it to occur. When training your dog, remember that when you change environments, you may have to re-teach him what you think he already knows. Ultimately, you must teach your dog in the setting where you would like your dog to perform the behavior.

Dogs Learn by Repetition, and Practice Makes Perfect

Dogs learn through repetition. The more often they engage in a certain behavior, the more likely they are to repeat it. Positive or negative, behavior patterns are likely to become habits. Practice makes perfect! If your dog performs a behavior once, the likelihood of his performing the behavior again is almost 100 percent. Be aware of this and try to divert any unwanted behaviors before they become patterns.

Summary

- Dogs are social. They do everything communally.

- Dogs live in the moment. They do not understand how your present behavior relates to a past event.

- Dogs are visual learners. Visual signals, your body language, and the inflection of your voice are the best ways to teach dogs quickly and easily.

- When being friendly, dogs will position themselves so that they are at an angle to each other, or they will stand, lie down, or sit next to each other.

- To dogs, property rights are determined by who has immediate possession of an item. If a dog has an object of yours, the dog does not consider it your property anymore.

- Dogs learn by association, i.e., by pairing things that occur simultaneously in the environment.

- Dogs are context learners and associate a new behavior with the environment in which you teach it to them. Ultimately, you must teach dogs in the settings in which you would like them to be able to perform the behavior.

- Dogs learn by repetition. Repeated behaviors are likely to become habits.

Chapter Two

Training Techniques

Passive Training and Problematic Behavior

Passive training is a wonderful form of training that teaches us patience and gives dogs rewarding opportunities to learn what it is that we want them to do. Passive training is a good way to train fearful and timid dogs, is nonthreatening to aggressive dogs, and is friendly and non-intimidating to submissive dogs. It is a great way to get a dog to look to you for guidance and to get a dog's mental wheels turning.

Essentially, passive training is waiting for a behavior that your dog naturally exhibits (even if only for a moment) and then reinforcing that behavior by rewarding it. It means having the patience to wait for a behavior that you want and then instantly reinforcing it through a reward and/or kudos the moment the behavior is performed. Through passive training, dogs learn that "you get what you want when you do what I want." You can passively train polite manners and behaviors in many ways. But you always want to set your dog up for success.

Let's say your dog wants to get outside. The moment you open the door, he rushes past you and almost topples you over. You can reward him for jumping at the door or for being quiet and remaining seated. If, as you open the door, he jumps on the door or dashes in front of you and you let him out, you are reinforcing jumping and dashing. On the other hand, if you wait for him to settle down, sit, and be calm before you open the door, then close it instantly when he begins to dash or jump for it, eventually he will learn that doors open when he sits and close when he tries to jump at them. It might take a little while (a day or two) to teach, but your dog will certainly sit the next time he wants you to open the door.

As you train your dog to sit quietly and wait for the door to open, the scenario may look like this: your dog wants to go outside and bounces up and down enthusiastically as you begin to open the door. Instead of opening the door, you wait. For an instant, he stops jumping and looks at you, so you begin to open the door. He begins to dash out. You close the door before he gets through it. Your dog is stunned (no, you didn't close the door on him!) and backs up a step. He may look at you and stay calm for another moment. You begin to open the door again, and again he dashes toward it. Before he gets through the door, you close it again. Your dog, a bit perplexed and frustrated, stops bouncing and looks at you. This time he may stop bouncing and remain staring at you for a few seconds. You smile (showing that he is doing what you want) and begin to open the door again. He hesitates and then begins to dash toward it. You close the door the instant he begins to make a run for it. Eventually, stupefied, he looks at you and sits. "Good dog!" you say and immediately let him outside. You have now just reinforced sitting as a behavior for getting the door to open. Then you can add additional specific behaviors: Walk to the door, make eye contact, sit, and wait. Voilà! The door opens. Of course, you can also just open the door and let your dog run exuberantly by. Just don't get angry at him for behaving in a way that you've been reinforcing all along.

The above is an example of passive training. A few repetitions and your dog will begin to figure out that when he is calm and not jumping at the door, you will open it for him. When he jumps and dashes to the door, you close it. He wants the door to open. So what will he do? Eventually he will sit calmly by the door while you open it. No other behavior seems to make you open the door. You could order him to sit, tell him to back up, or yell at him for dashing. Alternatively, through passive training (or "positive active" training), you can teach him from the start that all the goodies in life, such as doors opened, leashes removed, cookies, pats, belly rubs, the right to jump on the sofa, and playing with the tug toy come by way of showing polite manners. The moment your dog stops behaving calmly or politely, you stop giving him the goodies.

Gentleness, kindness, praise, baby talk, walks, food, playing with other dogs, playing with balls, car rides, running, attention, and the right to be on the bed are all things that your dog desires and finds rewarding. If you reward him by giving him these things for acting out, he will continue to act out. Why? Because acting out, i.e., exhibiting excessively hyperactive or overly zealous, mouthy, or jumpy behaviors, is being reinforced.

We often reinforce attention-seeking behaviors. Being social creatures, dogs think that any attention—providing it is not intensely negative—is better than no attention. To get your attention, which means getting your eye contact and interacting with you, your dog will exhibit a behavior that produces a reaction. If your dog engages in this behavior and you look at him (if only for a second), reprimand him, or focus on the behavior in any way, you reinforce it. Your dog wanted your attention, and you just gave it to him. He will do whatever works and will keep doing it, even if you hate it.

If, on the other hand, your dog performs a behavior that you don't like in order to get your attention and you immediately remove all eye contact and disengage from him, he will try to find another way to get your attention. This, of course, puts the responsibility on your shoulders. Does biting you in the butt work to get your attention, or will you react to him if he is calm and quiet?

We tend to focus on behaviors that we dislike in our dogs and ignore the behaviors that we like. When a dog does exactly what we want, we often overlook it. We are relieved that he didn't do something we didn't want. The moment that he performs a behavior that we find annoying, problematic emotionally draining, or frightening—barking, for instance—we reinforce this behavior by interacting with him. Reverse your tendency to obsess over and focus on the things that disturb you about your dog. React to him when he shows behaviors that you like. They are there. You just might be missing them. When your dog is quiet, do you gently say, "Good quiet," and pet him to acknowledge him for being quiet, before he begins barking? When your dog doesn't lunge at the car, do you acknowledge and reward him for being calm and looking at you instead? If your dog does not growl at you for walking by his bone while he is eating it, do you praise him and give him a treat?

A well-behaved, happy dog usually has a proactive, observant owner. (Or the owner was just very lucky to adopt a dog who is well-behaved regardless of the person's actions!) Obviously, training takes a lot of effort. Passive training is a way to reward and focus on behavior that you like without verbally or physically instructing your dog to do it.

Your dog figures out the behaviors that you are seeking on his own. These behaviors will soon become his default behaviors if they are reinforced consistently.

Shaping a Behavior

"Shaping a behavior" means achieving and reinforcing a behavior incrementally. Your dog may not show the exact behavior you are looking for, but he does at times exhibit behavior resembling the behavior you wish to see. "Shaping" means reinforcing any behavior closely resembling or approximating the behavior that you are looking for. Reinforcement means giving your dog something that will make him want to do the behavior again. Food is a good reinforcer for many dogs and is easy to work with.

"Successive approximation" is the best way to shape a behavior. You reward your dog for getting closer to the behavior that you are looking for. The closer the behavior resembles the desired behavior, the more you reward him, and you can then ask him to exhibit a little bit more of the behavior. He will perform behaviors that aren't the end behavior that you are looking for, but they will be close. Eventually, through shaping and gradual reinforcement with successive approximations, he will perform the exact desired behavior.

Complex behaviors such as heeling, weaving between a person's legs, turning on and off a light switch, putting toys in a toy basket, and rolling over are all behaviors that can be shaped. Teaching a dog to heel (i.e., stay by your side—whenever you turn, the dog turns with you and stops when you do) is teaching a high-level behavior. There are many steps and sequences a dog has to learn in order to heel. Dogs cannot learn to heel in one step like they can learn to sit on cue. Heeling involves more than one behavior. Eye contact, taking a step when you take a step, walking adjacent to you, stopping, turning with you—both to the right and to the left—are all separate behaviors that need to be taught individually.

When you break a behavior like heeling into its components, you see it isn't so simple. In order to teach your dog properly, you need to be aware of all the different individual behaviors that he needs to learn. If you do not build on a foundation, you and your dog will get lost as you try to progress.

Teaching a dog to heel by using a choke collar is not teaching a dog to voluntarily walk next to you, look at you, turn with you, or stay to one side of you. Using a choke collar is physically forcing a dog to stay by your side. To really learn a behavior, a dog must make the choice to exhibit that behavior from a range of alternatives. With a choke collar, a dog cannot choose one behavior over another. You cannot reinforce a behavior if there is only one behavior to reinforce. If your dog is on a choke collar and he proceeds ahead of you, he is jerked on his trachea. If he lags behind, he is tugged by a chain around his neck to make him catch up. "Leash pops" are serious business. You constrict a dog's airway. He will learn to avoid the jerk by staying next to your leg. From his perspective, this is the only option. He is not really learning to walk with you because you have taught him a different behavior. Those who rely on the choke collar and think that their dogs know how to heel should remove the choker and see whether their dogs can walk next to them without it. Even if they do, do these dogs really want to stay by their owners' sides, or are the dogs staying there because they are afraid of getting hurt?

You can shape many behaviors that you want your dog to exhibit. Fetching, for instance, is a behavior that can be shaped in a dog not accustomed to playing. If your dog seems to go after a ball but does not want to bring the ball back, you can shape the behavior (retrieving). As he runs to the ball, you praise him and maybe give him a treat. When he leaves the ball, you ignore him. If he then proceeds back to the ball, you reward him and encourage him every step of the way. Eventually, he may mouth the object. You reward him even more. By the time he has learned to pick up the toy, you can teach him to carry it through reward and reinforcement. Over time, you can teach him to carry the object and drop it on cue. You can then reward him for dropping the object closer to you, until finally he can drop the object in your hand.

Shaping a behavior is a good way to work with dogs without putting so much pressure on them that they fail to engage in the end behavior. If a behavior consists of many smaller foundational steps, dogs cannot perform the ultimate behavior the right way on the first try.

We also start "correcting" dogs for doing behaviors that we do not want before they even know what is expected of them. Focus on reinforcing any behaviors that you are seeking. Ignore those behaviors that you wish to discourage. If you focus on unwanted behaviors, you will just distract your dog with irrelevant information, and that will set you both up for failure. It is like teaching a child arithmetic. A child cannot learn how to add if the teacher only focuses on the child's mistakes and wrong answers. Focus on what your dog does right. You will find that those behaviors increase in frequency.

Luring

Luring is what most people think of as "bribing" a dog. Often, people fail to get beyond the luring stage during training. They then criticize the training technique. However, luring is a very important part of positive training. Luring is getting a dog to follow an object, including food. By teaching a dog to follow an object, you can build upon several foundational steps, move him through various positions, and teach him to execute the desired behavior.

Dogs are visual and will usually start to focus their attention on your hand or the object that you are holding. You can then turn any motion that you used to lure the dog into a hand-signal or verbal instruction. By having your dog follow something, whether it is food, a tennis ball, or a squeaky toy, you can move his body into certain positions or prompt him to follow a certain pattern. By moving him through the use of lures, you can teach him a sequence or position change without physical "prompting," which is the use of physical force to move a dog into a position. Pushing on a dog's shoulder blades to make him lie down is an example of physical prompting. Pulling him on a leash to make him come to you is another example of physical prompting.

Luring will produce similar or better results. Wherever you move the lure, your dog follows. Once he gets the idea, you can wean him off the lure by making it less visually obvious to him and then rewarding him in other ways. Eventually you can wean him off the lure entirely. Your dog follows a verbal prompt or a hand signal (or both), and you give him a reward that will make him repeat the behavior. There are many kinds of rewards. Food is just one of them. A reward is anything that your dog likes or finds fun to do.

Fig 5. Luring a sit
©2007 Lorraine Nicotera

There is a difference between bribery and luring. Most people bribe dogs. A good example of bribery is teaching a dog to sit for cookies. People hold up a cookie and say "Sit" and the dog sits (which he will do, because when dogs look up, their bottoms eventually hit the floor) and then they give the dog the cookie. When people are not asking the dog to sit, they are usually not showing the dog a cookie. Predictably, people always give cookies for sitting. Most dogs figure out quite quickly that when their hinies hit the ground, cookies appear.

However, if we teach dogs to sit for cookies, we usually fail to teach dogs to sit while we are opening doors or putting on or taking off leashes. We assume that dogs "know" what to do or how to "sit" because we taught them how to sit for cookies. But if you've never taught your dog to sit while you put on the leash, open a door, or throw a ball, he will never learn and most likely will not understand what you are asking.

Using a lure can help move your dog into a sitting position. You can then ask him to sit by using a lure while you put on his leash. While you put on the leash, you can reward him with the cookie you used to lure him. Then you can wean him off the cookie. The leash and walking outside become the reward. If you do not wean him off the lure, he will have a tough time doing the behavior without it. Your dog doesn't have to become a food junkie to be positively trained with food.

Active Training

"Active training" is what most people picture when training a dog: the use of a lure, prompt, or cue (physical, visual, or verbal) to encourage a dog to exhibit a behavior. Active training is the opposite of passive training. Passive training is when you wait for the dog to perform the behavior on his own and then you reinforce the behavior. Both techniques are used in positive training.

The following chapters teach you some basic exercises that can help you teach your dog positively and have fun at the same time. The aid of an experienced or qualified positive-oriented trainer can help you learn these exercises much more rapidly and effectively. Most hands-on training exercises are much easier to learn with the supervision or guidance of an instructor or in a small group class. Although positive trainers will share many of the same principles, every trainer has her own style and methods. In the back of this book there is a section on how to choose a trainer both you and your dog will like.

Summary

- "Passive training" means waiting for a behavior that your dog naturally exhibits—even if only for a moment—and then reinforcing that behavior by rewarding it. It involves having the patience to wait for a behavior you want and then instantly reinforcing it through rewards and/or praise the moment it happens.

- Passive training is good for fearful, timid, submissive, and aggressive dogs.

- Attention-seeking behaviors are actions that are specifically motivated by the desire for eye contact and interaction with you.

- If you reinforce a behavior, it will be repeated.

- "Shaping a behavior" means achieving and reinforcing behavior incrementally.

- "Successive approximation" is the best way to shape a behavior.

- Complex behaviors, such as heeling, weaving between a person's legs, turning a light switch on and off, and putting toys in a toy basket can all be shaped.

- Shaping a behavior is a good way to work with dogs without putting so much pressure on them that they fail to achieve the desired behavior.

- "Luring" is getting a dog to follow an object, including food. By teaching dogs to follow an object, you can then move them into different positions and teach them to perform specific behaviors.

- By getting dogs to move through the use of lures, you can teach them a sequence or position change without physical prompting.

- "Active training" is using a lure, prompt, or cue to encourage a dog to perform a behavior. In active training, you use physical, verbal, or visual instruction to prompt dogs to perform specific behaviors.

A Note on Teaching Puppies

There is no special consideration specifically to be given to puppies that should not or cannot be given to older dogs. In general, puppies can have shorter attention spans than older dogs. Short frequent training sessions are more productive than long arduous training regimes. In other words, a puppy might be able to enjoy 3-15 minutes of training and then enjoy some play time. Puppies are not good with endurance and require frequent bouts of play, sleep, mental stimulation, and eating.

Not all older dogs can pay attention for long periods. Similarly, some puppies can be fixated on something of interest for up to an hour. However, the rule for all positive training is to leave the dog or puppy wanting more. It is more effective to incorporate training into your day and to have 30 two to six minute training sessions, than it is to have one 30 minute training session.

There is no reason to wait before training a puppy. An eight week old puppy can certainly learn to come, look at you, leave objects, sit, give you a toy, and when taught positively, will love to do so.

All puppies should be fed three meals a day. There is a tendency for some people to underfeed puppies as they are afraid their puppy might gain weight. Puppies are little calorie burning machines. If your puppy seems frantic or hungry for food or treats, or becomes obsessive or hyper when you are eating, your puppy may need to eat more. Sometimes excess hyperactivity can be caused because your puppy is too hungry. Giving bigger regular meals seems to help puppies relax and settle down.

You can teach and train your puppy with doggy kibble, but stay away from heavily processed food or treats with artificial colors and a lot of by-products. Avoid treats containing a lot of sugar, corn syrup, and corn meal. Instead stick with treats that contain grains such as oats or brown rice.

Chapter Three

Training Exercises

Attention

Getting a dog's attention is very important. If you can't get your dog's attention, you won't get much else. Frequently, we call our dogs' names and make eye contact with them. Then we lose the connection. When you call your dog's name, he will look at you, but then he looks away and continues to do what he was previously doing. When he is looking at you, he is asking, "What do you want?" If you miss or don't acknowledge his eye contact, he will think that you didn't know what you wanted or that his name doesn't mean anything.

Getting your dog's attention means that you can call him by his name and he looks at you or in your direction. This behavior can be shaped and is particularly good for dogs who are afraid of making eye contact or who avoid eye contact entirely.

Do's

- Do call your dog by his name only when you have his attention or you know you will get it. Don't set yourself up for failure by becoming a broken record.

- Do use your dog's name in a positive way. If he senses stress or frustration, he may avoid making eye contact.

- Do use inflection when trying to get your dog's attention. Noises that naturally get dogs' attention are high-pitched and vary (i.e., whistles, claps, smoochy kisses).

- Do make calling your dog's name relevant to him! When he hears his name, something should follow that relates to him. Remember, his name is his identity; it doesn't give him any instructions.

- Do say your dog's name louder and more clearly and add some noises or sounds if you cannot get his attention. If you *still* cannot get his attention, keep trying, but do *not* use his name. The more you repeat his name without any relevance, the *less* likely it becomes that he will pay attention to you.

Don'ts

- Don't try to get your dog's attention by using his name unless you are fairly certain to get it.

- Don't use your dog's name as a replacement for the instruction "Come."

- Don't use your dog's name when you mean to say "No." Just as a dog's name does not mean "Come," it does not mean "No."

- Don't use your dog's name in a negative context or when you are angry. He will avoid making eye contact and may become anxious upon hearing his name.

- Don't repeat your dog's name over and over again hoping for a different result if you cannot get his attention after calling his name the first time. Try using other ways to get his attention.

An Attention Exercise

This exercise is a way to shape eye contact and to establish a positive association for your dog between your looking at him and his looking back at you. Once you can visually cue him to make eye contact, you can add a verbal prompt by pairing it with his behavior. He will learn that this prompt means to look at you.

Sit or kneel opposite your dog so that he is facing you. Give him a treat if he is sitting, although he does not have to sit for this exercise. Hold a food treat in your hand. Show him the treat, then draw your hand up toward your eyes. Pause there for a second or two. Then bring your hand next to your head, with the tips of your fingers touching the back of your ear. All dogs will initially look at the hand holding the food. They will not look into your eyes. *Wait.* Do not prompt or encourage him to look at you. The instant he does, give him the treat. This is passive training. Keep repeating this exercise until your dog can give you steady eye contact. When he can look at you eight or nine times out of 10 before looking back at the food treat in your hand, increase the length of time he looks at you. To increase duration, simply delay giving the treat by one or two seconds. If your dog looks away, you may be going too fast. Once he can look at you and maintain eye contact for two seconds or longer, speak his name a second before signaling for eye contact.

Fig 6. *Drawing Lucy's attention to my eyes.*
©2007 Margaret Crow

Fig 7. *Waiting for eye contact.*
©2007 Margaret Crow

If you have difficulty determining whether or not your dog is looking at you, move your hand a few inches away from your ear so that you can see his eyes shift. Keep your hand still. The object of the exercise is to have your dog focus on your eyes and not on your hand. If you move your hand too frequently, it will become distracting.

Say your dog's name. Right after saying his name, add the word "look" or "watch." When your dog looks at you, immediately give him the treat.

Your dog will always look back at the treat once he makes eye contact with you. Initially, you are only asking him to make eye contact with you for a few seconds, so it is OK for him to look back at the treat.

Always hold the food next to or behind your ear, as opposed to in front of your body or in front of your face. Your dog will eventually look away from the food to look at your eyes. If you hold the food treat in front of your eyes, it will look as if he is looking at you when he is actually looking at the food.

Once your dog can perform the attention exercise in one room, change rooms. Then change locations. Do the exercise outside in a quiet setting. Change your body position. Ask for his attention while standing, sitting on the sofa, and so on. Always begin this exercise in areas with few distractions. When adding distractions or when outside, decrease the amount of time that you ask him to look at you for and use more desirable rewards.

Recall

A "recall"—training lingo for coming when called—takes place when your dog, after being away from you, approaches you again upon receiving a designated hand or verbal signal. There may be times when you have to physically go and get him. This is to be expected, but this is not a recall. Running after your dog and chasing him does not encourage him to come to you.

Do's

- Do teach your dog the meaning of your recall signal. Call him with your designated prompt or cue when he is already coming to you or when you know that he will approach you.

Fig 8. Calling Kiva to "Come" as she is retrieving.
©2007 Kerri Fenn

- Do run or move *away* from your dog if you want him to come to you! His natural inclination will be to follow you. He will not learn to approach or follow you if you are chasing or following him.

- Do walk, move, and orient your body in the direction that you want your dog to go. If you face him and look at what he is doing or looking at, he will be less likely to pay attention to you because you are not giving him any clear guidance or instruction.

Fig 9. Walking away from Jake so he will follow me.
©2007 Lauren MacDonald

- Do use high-pitched noises and change the inflection in your voice (i.e., baby talk, squeaks, whistles, smoochy kisses, claps) to get your dog's attention. "Let's go" and "I'm leaving" are two expressions that go up and down in pitch as we say them. Dogs tend to tune out monotonous sounds.

- Do position yourself with your back toward your dog, kneel down, and call him if he is fearful, hesitant, or timid. A hesitant dog will approach you if he feels that you are not threatening. We face dogs when we want to block their movements or teach them to stay. If you do face your dog, walk *away* from him as you call him, unless you are teaching him a formal recall through training exercises. When he leaves you temporarily, he is not running away from you permanently but is preoccupied with something else. More than likely, he *will* want to come back to you. He just wants to do something else first. The more distractions there are in your dog's environment, the more enticing you have to be when you want him to come to you.

Fig 10. Kneeling away from Jake to encourage him to approach.
©2007 Lauren MacDonald

- Do encourage your dog the entire time that he is in the process of coming to you. You can easily lose his interest as he approaches you. If you are too boring, he will find something else more stimulating to do.

- Do kneel down as your dog comes to you and avoid leaning forward or reaching over him with outstretched arms, especially if he is fearful or shy.

- Do praise and reward your dog profusely when he gets to you. Rewards can be food-based or activities he enjoys, such as running or playing tug-of-war.

- Do call your dog to come to you, make his recall rewarding, and then let him go back to what he was doing previously. By releasing your dog after he has come to you and you have rewarded him, you are telling him that coming to you is a positive experience and not just a way to end play or to indicate that an activity that he enjoys is over.

Don'ts

- Don't call your dog with your designated signal unless he is approaching you or you know he will come to you.

- Don't chase or follow your dog if you want him to approach you or come to you.

- Don't stand or lean directly over your dog, or face him if you want him to come to you.

- Do not punish your dog for coming to you by using it as an opportunity to reprimand or scold him or to end social interactions or play.

- Do not call your dog with your signal if you are going to do something that he doesn't like, such as clip his nails or give him a bath.

Recall Exercises

The principles of recall can be taught through games that help your dog learn your signal. Be sure to use your "Come" signal in situations other than the games. If you only use your "Come" signal when playing the games, your dog will not generalize the signal to other situations. Remember, dogs learn in the environments and in the contexts that you teach them.

One-Person Game

If you play this game on light surfaces, you will need dark treats, and vice versa. Your dog needs to be able to find the treats quickly and easily. If you play on grass or patterned carpets, he will have to spend too much time trying to find the treats. Play this game on hard surfaces, such as tile or wooden floors, sidewalks, driveways, or tennis courts.

Teach your dog a hand signal before you teach him the game. Your hand signal does not have to become a formal signal. You are going to use your hand as a target—something visual for your dog to follow.

Imagine a ½-inch length of string running between your dog's nose and your hand. Wherever you move your hand, his nose should follow. With food in your hand, place the back of your hand toward your dog's nose and lure him to you by pulling your hand toward your body. Once he gets to you, give him the treat. Do this until he can approach you by following your hand without a food lure. Once he follows your hand, you can begin the game.

Hold a bunch of treats in one hand or keep treats with you in a training pouch. Stand facing your dog. Toss a food treat on the floor about 1 foot away from you. Don't throw the treat over your dog's head; he will lose track of it. When he gets the treat, hold another treat in your hand and lure him back to you. Instead of giving him the treat when he gets to you, toss it again.

Continue to toss the food treats, increasing the distance with each throw and luring your dog back to you each time with another treat. Believe it or not, when you throw a food treat your dog will not immediately come back to you for more. Most dogs just sniff the floor, hoping more treats will rain from the sky. Once your dog understands the game and starts coming back to you after each throw without your having to lure him, add a verbal signal: his name followed by your "Come" prompt. Say your dog's name, followed by your signal, when he is almost done eating the food treat or has just finished. He will come to you after you call him. It will look as if he is obeying your verbal prompt, although at this point he is just following the rules of the game.

Fig 11-13. Playing the one person recall game with Lucy.
©2007 Margaret Crow

Once your dog comes to you reliably after each throw, put your hands behind your back. Use only your verbal signal. If he is already looking at you and paying attention to you and he approaches you, you do not need to say his name. Just use your "Come" prompt to reinforce the behavior.

The focus of this exercise is not for your dog to run after the food, but for him to come to you. If you throw the food too far away in the early stages of the game or before your dog has gotten to you, he may not come back to you all the way after each throw. Wait for him to get to you before you throw the treat again. If he does not come to you, repeat his name and your "Come" signal once, add some prompts, and immediately use your hand signal to encourage him to come to you. Then toss the food treat when he comes to you.

If your dog plays fetch and can bring objects back to you and then release the object for you to throw again, you have a recall game! Call your dog with your signal by saying his name and your "Come" prompt every time he gets the object and heads back in your direction.

Once your dog understands this game, play it in many environments. Begin using your signal in real-life situations when he is at short distances from you. Follow a two-to-three call rule: Call your dog to come to you once. If he doesn't come, wait for a moment, then say his name louder, more clearly, and add high-pitched noises. The instant he looks at you, move in the opposite direction or move in the direction you want him to follow you. If he does not come to you the second time you call, do whatever you can to get him to approach you. You may have to go to him and put the leash on him, but don't keep repeating his name or your "Come" prompt. Otherwise, he will become desensitized to both.

Start preceding all enjoyable activities—when you know your dog will approach—with your designated "Come" signal. This will not only help to reinforce your signal, but it will also make coming to you a positive experience for him.

After you say your dog's name, do not wait too long before adding your "Come" signal or he will look at you but not know what you want from him. He will then quickly lose interest and you will be forced to try to get his attention all over again.

Two-Person Game

Since the one-person game teaches a dog the body language and voice of the caller, it is always good for both people playing the two-person game to play the one-person game first.

Have ready treats that your dog will enjoy. Stand about 4 feet away from your partner so that you each can be within an arm's reach of your dog. Lure him to come to you with a food treat. When he comes to you, give him the treat. Then the other player steps in and lures your dog to come. When your dog goes to that person, she delivers a treat.

Once your dog understands the game and will run back and forth between players for food treats, add your verbal signal. Say his name and immediately follow it with your "Come" prompt while you lure him to you with your hand motion or the treat. Increase the distance between you and your partner as your dog gets better at playing the game. When your dog catches on to the game, there will be no need to lure him. Then you can focus on your verbal prompt. If your dog regresses and stops coming to you when you stop using your hand signal, decrease the distance between you and your partner. You may have stopped using your hand motion or the lure too soon. If you increase the distance too quickly, a dog will usually stay by one person and the game will deteriorate.

Fig 14-15. Playing a two person recall game.
©2007 Margaret Crow

Once your dog understands that the game consists of running back and forth between two people for goodies, you will need a signal to let your partner know when it is her turn to call, especially when you are at a distance from each other or in locations where you can't see each other. Say a word or expression such as "Perfect" or "Good job" after you give him the food treat. This way, your partner will know when it is her turn to call, and you won't end up calling your dog at the same time or before any treats have been delivered. This additional verbal cue also lets your dog know that it is time to race back to the other person.

Do not repeat your dog's name or call him over and over again if he does not pay attention or come to you. Add a prompt, such as a whistle or a hand clap, and then use your hand signal to lure him to you.

Hide-and-Seek

Once your dog can play the two-person game, you can play hide-and-seek with him. Your dog can get treats and be rewarded for finding people. When teaching your dog this game, don't make hiding places too difficult at first. "Hide" in a place where he can see you. This is a great game for kids and dogs to play together. Many dogs love playing hide-and-seek.

Begin by holding your dog; this will make him want to follow the person who hides. Eventually you can teach him to sit and stay or wait next to you until the other person calls. The other player hides and calls him. When your dog finds this person, she celebrates with your dog. Your dog can run around, receive treats, or play tug-of-war. When this person is done rewarding your dog, she holds him and gives you a verbal signal to let you know that it is your turn. Hide and call your dog with your signal. When he finds you, celebrate. It is up to you how you reward your dog. Do something that he enjoys.

When your dog understands that the object of the game is to find the caller, you can increase the distance between players and make your hiding places more challenging.

More Recall Games

Once your dog is good at the previous two recall games and the game of hide-and-seek, you can play other games to reinforce his recall.

Three-Person Game

If there are more than two people in your family, you can add a third player to the two-person recall game. This can be helpful if your dog needs to learn to come to different people.

All players should begin the game close enough to each other that they can use their hand signal or lure your dog to them if necessary. Each person calls your dog to come with the designated signal and then rewards him for coming. Distance can be increased between players once your dog understands the principles of the game. Be sure to agree on a praise word that each person can use to indicate to another player that it is her turn to call your dog. This word should be said after your dog gets rewarded on each call. If you don't use this additional praise word, people may call your dog while he is in the middle of chewing the treat—dogs don't seem to listen well while chewing—or before you have finished delivering the treat. "Great job" or "Perfect" are good choices.

Teach Your Dog to Listen to the Verbal Signal

The one-person and the two-person recall games teach your dog a pattern of behavior. The one-person game teaches him to get a treat or an object and then return to you for more. The two-person game teaches him to run back and forth between people to get rewards. After teaching him these patterns you can add a word or signal meaning "Come" and he will associate this signal with coming to you. Since dogs love patterns, most dogs simply follow the rules of the game without listening to your "Come" signal. This game teaches your dog to *listen* for your verbal prompt before coming to you. Some dogs are naturally very good at this. Others need to improve their listening skills.

Call your dog using your verbal "Come" signal. When he gets to you, give him a treat. Praise him after you give him the treat. The other person playing then calls him. When your dog comes to that person, she delivers praise and a treat. If your dog races to either you or the other player before either of you have used your signal, do not give him a treat. If your dog happens to run to you before you call him, the other player can call him again.

Increase the distance between players as your dog gets better at playing the game. Be sure to add a second verbal signal after you give your dog a treat to let other players know when it is their turn to call him.

Playing a Recall Game While You Distract Your Dog

Two people are needed for this game. One person intentionally distracts your dog. You are the caller and you do not have any toys or treats; the person who distracts your dog should have all the goodies, but should not give him any treats or toys.

Call your dog with your designated signal. The person you are playing with tries to mildly distract your dog. Since your dog is being distracted, he will likely ignore you. Keep calling and using prompts, whistling, or running in the opposite direction; do anything that you can think of to get your dog to approach you. If your dog comes to you, the person who has the treats or toys either runs over and gives your dog a treat or tosses a toy to you so that you can play with your dog. By running up to you to give your dog a treat, the treat-bearer distracts your dog again, and you can call your dog to come to you once more. When your dog comes to you, the other person once again runs to deliver a treat or gives you a toy so that you can play with him. Your dog will learn that the only way to get a reward is to listen to you—the caller—and to leave the person who is distracting him. Always praise your dog and give him better rewards for recalls in the face of distractions. You can vary the rules of this game as you and your dog get better at playing it.

When your dog gets good at this game, you can make it more difficult by only giving him treats when he responds just to your verbal signal. At this stage, if your dog rushes over to you *before* being called (again, dogs catch on to patterns quickly), don't give him a treat. The object of the game is not just to come to you, but to come to you specifically when you use your designated verbal signal.

Do not move on to new games too quickly. If you keep adding new rules and standards for your dog to follow before he has learned the basics, he will soon become confused, get frustrated, and stop playing with you.

A variation: You can vary this game by playing a two-person recall game with the person your dog least attends to. When your dog comes to the caller, the caller praises him and gives lots of fantastic rewards. The person whom the dog is most responsive to also rewards the dog for listening to the caller.

One-Person/Two-Toy Game

This is a good game for dogs who do not carry toys around but like to chase them and for dogs who have not been taught to drop objects.

Use two or three identical toys that your dog loves, such as stuffed toys, tennis balls, or tug toys. Stand in the middle of an open area. If you do not want your dog off-leash, use a long-line or keep him on an extra long leash. Show him a toy and throw it for him. Just as he gets to the toy, get his attention and wave an identical toy. Then run away from him. Enthusiastically call him to come to you using your designated signal. As soon as your dog comes to you, stop running and throw the toy that you are holding in the opposite direction of that in which you threw the first toy. As he runs by you to get the newly thrown toy, pick up the toy you threw originally and wave it again and call him to come to you using your designated signal. Keep repeating this pattern, calling him every time. Once your dog learns this game, you can vary it by teaching him to drop the toy, so that he drops one toy right at your feet and then runs after a newly tossed toy. This is a wonderful way to exercise your dog, reinforce a recall, and teach him a "Give" command or a "Thank you" (giving him a treat for releasing a toy).

Target Game

This game is for dogs who are not very toy-motivated or who don't know how to play, such as many abused or rescued dogs. Your dog must be clicker-trained, as you will teach him to touch an object or ball by using a clicker. If your dog is sound-sensitive, you can condition him to another noise or verbal marker.

Start with a toy, a ball, or an object that your dog likes. Show him the toy. When he touches the toy with either his nose or his paws, click and give him a treat. Increase the distance between yourself and the toy. Your dog should go to the toy, touch it, and then come back to you for a food reward. Click as he touches the toy. Then call him back to you with your designated signal. The object of the game is for your dog to touch the ball or toy and come back to you for a treat. The game will look like fetch, except that your dog will not bring the toy back to you. Instead, you will have to get the toy and toss it so that he can run to it, touch it with his nose, and then run back to you.

Summary

- Always use your dog's name positively.

- Change the inflection in your voice and use high-pitched noises to get a dog's attention.

- Make calling your dog's name relevant to him. When he hears his name, something should happen that relates to him.

- Don't use your dog's name if you are going to do something that he dislikes.

- Your dog's name does not mean "No" or "Come."

- If you want your dog to approach you, run or walk in the opposite direction.

- Always reward your dog when he comes after you call him.

- Don't chase your dog if you want him to come to you.

- Don't punish your dog or do something that he dislikes after he comes to you.

- Sometimes you may need to get your dog. Don't call him to come to you while you are trying to catch him.

Sit, Stand, and Down

"Sit," "Stand," and "Down" are verbal signals that indicate body positions. A standing position is that in which your dog is standing on all fours. When your dog lies down he is in the "down" position. There are two down positions: a "relaxed down" and a "posed down." A posed down is the position in which your dog looks like a sphinx. A relaxed down is the position in which he is leaning in one direction or is favoring one hip over the other.

You must teach your dog two sitting positions: sitting in front of you and sitting next to you. Picture yourself on a walk with your dog. When you meet someone you may want your dog to sit next to you. Keep in mind that dogs learn exactly what you teach them. If you always teach your dog to sit in front of you, he will always face you when he sits. If you then ask him to sit next to you, he will pivot to sit in front of you. This can be problematic for people who want to teach their dogs to sit next to them before crossing the street. They stop at a curb and ask their dogs to sit; their dogs comply by walking partially onto the road to sit in front of them.

It is also important to teach your dog to sit or lie down in many locations—especially in the specific locations and situations in which you would like him to sit. Teach your dog to sit and lie down in the car. In addition, teach him to sit or lie down for non-food rewards, such as opening doors (including car doors, if he likes car rides), taking off the leash, running and playing with other dogs, and being petted. If your dog is an older dog or has trouble with his hips, ask for a behavior that is easy on the joints, such as looking at you or waiting.

Sit

Hold a piece of food in front of your dog's nose. He may nibble or lick your hand. This is OK. Imagine a ½-inch length of string running between his nose and your hand. Lift your hand up slightly, making a little arc from the bottom of you dog's chin to the top of his forehead. He should sit by following your hand. If you hold the treat too high, he will just jump or stare at you. If he seems to be moving around a lot, more than likely your hand is moving around a lot. Keep your hand steady. When he moves his head up, his rear should hit the floor. The moment your dog sits, praise him and give him the treat.

Fig 16. Sit signal.
©2007 Margaret Crow

When your dog begins to anticipate your hand motion, wean him off seeing the treat. Keep your hand flat while holding the treat. You can hold the treat under your thumb or between your fingers with your palm facing up. Make an upward motion with your hand. When your dog sits, give him the treat. When you can use a flat hand to instruct him to sit, start delivering treats with your other hand. You are now using a hand signal. Reward your dog profusely for sitting without being lured by food.

The next step is to put the food in your pocket. Show your dog your empty hands. Ask him to sit with your hand signal. He may hesitate. Wait. When he sits, give him a handful of treats. Say "Sit" if you think he will sit with your hand signal. By pairing the verbal signal with your dog's behavior, you are teaching him the meaning of your signal. Always keep training sessions short and sweet. End on a good note.

Stand

When your dog is sitting, hold a treat in front of his nose with the palm of your hand facing him. Pull your arm back in one straight motion to the side of your leg or in front of your leg as you take a step back. Your dog will stand to follow the food. Immediately give him the treat. You can then lure him back to a sitting position by moving your hand slightly over his head. When he sits, give him a treat. Keep repeating this by rewarding your dog for each position change. When he catches on,

Fig 17. *Bringing Lucy to a standing position.*
©2007 Margaret Crow

Fig 18. *Teaching sit from the side.*
©2007 Margaret Crow

hide the food in your hand by placing the treat under your thumb or between your fingers and use a flat hand to signal him. When making a formal hand signal, remember to deliver treats from your other hand. Add a verbal cue when you know your dog will stand upon seeing your hand signal.

Sit From the Side

With your dog standing next to you, position him between yourself and a barrier such as a wall, sofa, chair, or tree. Put food in front of his nose and lure him into a sitting position by making a little arc from the bottom of his chin to the top of his head. By positioning him between yourself and a wall or another barrier, you can prevent him from rotating to sit in front of you. Alternate luring your dog to stand, then sit, then stand again. Reward him for each position change. Keep your arm close to your body when luring him to sit next to you. If your hand is too far in front of you, he will sit in front of you—not next to you. Once your hand motion is enough to prompt him to sit, wean him off the food lure. Start hiding the food from him. Add your verbal cue when you know he will sit upon seeing your hand signal.

Down

It is easier to teach your dog to lie down when he is already sitting. Have patience if you have a little dog or a dog with very long or very short legs. It can be challenging for all dogs to understand what it is that you want from them. Once your dog understands you, you should have little difficulty instructing him to lie down.

Position your dog on a comfortable surface, such as a rug or a dog bed (with little dogs, you can practice on a bed or a sofa). Start when your dog is in a sitting position. Hold a food treat in your hand and put your hand under your dog's nose with your open palm facing the floor. Bring your hand gently down to the floor. Your dog may lick or paw at your hand or get confused and lick your face for a moment. Wait patiently. The instant he lies down give him a handful of treats or a particularly desirable treat. Bring him out of the "down" position by luring him to stand or sit. Alternate luring him to sit and lie down. You can also lure him to stand, ask him to sit, and then lure him to lie down again. Add the word "Down" when you know that he will lie down with the lure or by following your hand motion.

Fig 19. Luring a down.
©2007 Margaret Crow

You can shape lying down for dogs who have difficulty. Place your dog on a soft comfortable surface, such as a rug or dog bed. Ask him to sit. Hold a piece of food in front of his nose and bring your hand gently to the floor. Give your dog treats continually as he follows your hand. Stop giving him treats before he stands or sits up. Eventually he will lie down all the way. Have patience. Shaping a down may take a few practice sessions. Give your dog a handful of treats when he finally lies down. Always keep training sessions short and sweet.

Summary

- Teach your dog to sit next to you and in front of you.

- Teach your dog to sit and lie down in different locations.

- When teaching your dog to lie down, provide a soft surface, such as a rug, carpet, or dog bed for him to lie down on.

- Wean your dog off the food lure by hiding it from him. You can do this by placing food under your thumb or between your fingers while you lure him into position.

- Turn the hand motion you use to lure your dog into a hand signal.

- When your dog regularly follows your hand signal, give him treats with your other hand.

- Add your verbal cue when you know that you can signal him to sit or lie down.

- Replace food rewards with nonfood rewards, such as doors opening, putting on or taking off the leash, or throwing toys for your dog to chase.

Leave It and Thank You

Dogs have a simple notion of ownership. In dog culture, if an object is in your paws or in your mouth, it's yours. If no one possesses an object, ownership is determined by who is closest to that object or who gets to it first. Many misunderstandings take place between people and dogs when it comes to property and ownership. From a dog's perspective, if you aren't holding, working with, or eating an object, it's not yours.

This can cause problems for puppies and new dogs. We frequently reprimand dogs for stealing socks, wallets, pillows, stuffed animals, tissue or toilet paper, remote controls, or food left out on the table. We try to take these items away from dogs and then wonder why these dogs avoid us, growl, or clamp their jaws down on the object so that we can't pry it out of their mouths.

Dogs tend not to take things directly from each other's mouths. It is rude. But people constantly take things from dogs' mouths and assume dogs know that these items belong to us. From your dog's point of view, an item on the floor or on the sidewalk is not yours to tell him to leave alone. Likewise, if he picks up an object and you try to take it out of his mouth, he will resist you because you have no right to take it. If an item is of high value to your dog, he may growl at you when you approach him. In his view, you have no rights to it—unless, of course, he *wants* to give it to you.

The more your dog values an item, the more difficult it will be for him to give it to you. If you punish or reprimand him for taking an object, he will grow afraid of you and several things may happen: he will try to scarf down the object when you are not looking (common sense on his part); he will see you coming and gobble the item down quickly; he may growl at you for your rude behavior to tell you to back off; or he will run away from you. The best way to teach your dog to abandon an object or give it to you is by teaching him that it's rewarding to do so. Dogs do not want to give away what rightfully belongs to them. However, you can teach your dog to feel good about giving you his belongings.

Leave It

The beginning stage of this exercise teaches your dog to back away from an object that you have in your hands. Once he understands your cue to "Leave it," you can make this exercise more challenging by holding more valuable objects or by lowering your hand to the ground. Ultimately you will leave the items on the floor. This exercise is messy at first, but dogs love it and learn it quickly.

Hold a food treat in your hand and make a fist. Present your fist to your dog and allow him to lick and paw at your hand. Do not pull your hand away from him or you will encourage him to follow it. Don't say anything. You are teaching him to "Leave it" passively. Your dog will learn that he gets what he wants when he does what it is that you want him to, which is to not lick or paw at your hand. Give him the treat the

Fig 20. Leave it exercises.
©2007 Margaret Crow

46

moment he stops nudging or pawing at you. He might only be getting ready to nudge or paw at you again, but through repetition and good timing on your part he will realize that he gets the food by moving his nose away from your hand. After a series of repetitions, your dog should back away from your hand or simply watch it politely when you present the treat. Once he no longer nudges or paws you, say "Leave it" in a nice tone of voice as you show him your fist. Praise and reward him when he backs away from the treat. By pairing the words "leave it" with your dog's behavior you are teaching him the meaning of the verbal signal. If your dog still nudges your fist with his nose when you present the treat, do not add your verbal cue. Wait until he is demonstrating the behavior that you want him to before you start labeling it verbally.

Once your dog starts backing away from your fist and responding to your cue to "Leave it," make the exercise a little bit more challenging by holding the food under your thumb in an open palm. Position your hand next to your dog's face but not under his nose or chin. (If you

Fig 21. Leave it exercises.
©2007 Margaret Crow

hold the food under his nose, he will think you are offering him the treat because this is how you position your hand when you are feeding him.) Your dog will probably lick or paw at your hand again. When he backs away or stops licking or pawing at you, give him the treat. Say "Leave it" when he leaves the food that you present to him.

Once your dog understands that he needs to back away from your hand you can start to increase the amount of time that he has to wait. Ask him to "Leave it" for a few seconds longer with each presentation. If he starts to nudge you again, you may be waiting too long. You want your dog to succeed. Continue this exercise until he leaves the food in your open hand with every presentation. Then start rewarding him with treats from your other hand the hand not presenting the food. Your dog is now being rewarded for completely leaving the food presented in your hand.

Always give your dog more treats or a better treat than the one he is leaving in your hand. To increase the difficulty of this exercise, gradually lower your hand to the floor. Then place the food treat on the floor. Once the food is on the floor, lure him away from the food with another treat. Say "Leave it" when he leaves the treat on the ground. Reward him for not touching the treat or backing away from it. If you see him going for the treat, cover it with your hand or foot. When he backs away from the treat say "Leave it," pause, and reward him. Don't go too fast or try to make this exercise too difficult at first. Set your dog up for success.

Please don't reprimand your dog when he touches or paws at your hand. He will not automatically understand what it is that you want. Give him a bunch of treats or some very good treats for especially good behaviors. It is easier to start by giving him treats with the same hand that is holding the food. Once you are comfortable holding the food under your thumb or in your open palm, begin giving your dog treats with your other hand. You are now rewarding him for leaving the food in your hand entirely alone.

Fig 22. Leave it exercises.
©2007 Margaret Crow

Fig 23. Leave it exercises.
©2007 Margaret Crow

49

Thank You, Drop, or Give

"Thank you" is what you say when you take away an object that your dog already has. Start with items that are of little value to your dog or that you don't mind him having. Toys, sticks, and balls are good objects to begin with. When your dog plays with a toy or carries an object, put a piece of food in front of his nose. Extend your hand and say "Thank you" as you take the item from him, give him the treat, and then give him back the object. He may follow you for more treats, but don't give them to him. Only give him treats when you take something from him, and always give him something better than the object that you have taken away. Then give him back the object he originally had. Once he begins to release or offer his objects to you, phase out the food lure by hiding the treat in your hand or putting it in your pocket. Extend your hand, say, "Thank you," and take the object. Give him abundant goodies and remember to give the object back to him. Eventually you will be able to take something from your dog even if you are not going to return it. "Thank you" is a great exercise to teach puppies.

Summary

- Dogs have a simple notion of ownership. If no one is eating, touching, or directly holding an object, ownership is determined by who is closest to the object or who gets to it first.

- The more valuable an item is to your dog, the more challenging it will be for him to relinquish it.

- Dogs tend not to remove things from each other's mouths.

- The best way to teach your dog to leave an object or give it to you is by teaching him that it is rewarding to do so.

- Punishing your dog for taking an item will make him afraid of you and will either cause him to run away from you with the object or encourage him to take things when you aren't looking.

- When teaching your dog to give things to you, take an object away from him, give him a special food treat, and then give him back the object.

Stay

Teaching a dog to "Stay" happens gradually. When you give your dog positive reinforcement for sitting or lying down for a specified amount of time, during distractions, and as you walk away from him, you are teaching him to stay. You must first teach him to sit, stand, or lie down on cue in the settings you want him to "Stay" before you begin stay training.

Begin by teaching your dog to sit, stand, or lie down for a specified length of time. Start with a few seconds. Once he can reliably stay in a sit, stand, or down position for a certain length of time (30-60 seconds), you can then put distance between yourself and your dog—or you can stay next to him and add mild distractions. As always, set him up for success. Start with short intervals and don't ask him to stay for too long or increase the distance between the two of you too quickly.

You must also teach your dog a release word: a word that tells him that you expect nothing more of him and he is free to do as he pleases. By teaching him a release word, you will avoid teaching him that the food reward you give him means that he no longer needs to engage in the behavior that you are asking for. If you don't teach your dog a release word, the food will become the end goal and will no longer work to reinforce a behavior. Over time, this becomes bribery. This can cause a jack-in-the-box response. A dog lies down, is given a treat and then he pops back up again. By teaching your dog a release word, he will learn that treats and rewards do not mean that he is finished perfoming a behavior but that he is doing a terrific job at that behavior. If you do not teach him a release word he will have no way of knowing how long you would like him to stay for. He will become confused and his behavior will become unreliable. Make it clear when you want your dog to perform a behavior and when he is free to do as he likes.

Ask your dog to sit or lie down. Do not reward him. If he does not know how to sit or lie down on cue you are not ready to teach him to stay. Say "Stay" as you give your dog treats. Then say your release word (i.e., "free," "OK," "finished") and stop giving him treats. Walk away from him or turn your back on him. He will probably get up and walk around or follow you. This is fine. A few minutes later, ask him to sit or lie down again. Again, say "Stay" and give him treats the entire time that he remains in the position that you asked for. Speak your release word and stop giving him treats. Increase the time interval between giving treats as your dog gets better at lying down or sitting for extended periods of time. Stop giving him treats when you release him.

If your dog breaks the "stay," immediately get him back into a "sit" or "down" position and start over. If you find yourself frequently starting over, decrease the amount of time that you ask him to sit or lie down for or you may need to limit the distractions around him.

When you first start adding distractions to the exercise, stand next to your dog. Reward him with treats during and immediately following a distraction. Eventually you will only deliver treats after the distraction has passed. Then you can release him. Remember to use better rewards and decrease the amount of time that you expect him to stay for when you increase the distance between you and your dog or add distractions.

Fig 24. Teaching Kiva to stay from the front.
©2007 Kerri Fenn

Fig 25. Teaching Kiva to stay while a car passes.
©2007 Kerri Fenn

To teach your dog to stay when you are at a distance from him, think of yourself as a bungee cord. Ask him to sit or lie down. Tell him to "Stay" and take a step away from him. Then step back to him and give him a treat. Repeat this pattern several times and then release him.

Fig 26. Teaching Kiva to stay while I face away from her.
©2007 Kerri Fenn

Distance Training

It is not terribly difficult to teach your dog to respond to your requests from a distance. Start with an exercise that you have already taught him. Stand very close to him when you begin the exercise. When he performs the desired behavior reliably, take a step back. You can tether him or keep him behind a baby gate to keep him from following you as you back away. But don't back away or increase the distance between the two of you too quickly. Otherwise, you may confuse him. If your dog seems perplexed or doesn't perform the behavior you ask for, step closer to him and ask him again. When he performs the behavior reward him profusely. Once you step away from him and ask him to perform a desired behavior, he will anticipate that you will return to him to give him a reward.

Another person can also give your dog treats for following your requests. This person should remain beside your dog at all times so that she can give him treats. Your dog can be on a leash to keep him from following you as you back away. You should not have any treats on you. Begin by standing next to your dog and ask him to perform a behavior. When he complies, the person helping you gives him a treat. Gradually increase the distance between yourself and your dog. The person giving him treats should give him better or more treats when your dog responds to your requests from farther away.

The Crazy Human and Dog Game

This is a great game to teach your dog because it reinforces all the behaviors you've already taught him and teaches him to listen to you even when he is excited. The object of the game is to reward your dog with play for listening to your instructions.

You can be creative when playing this game. Ask your dog to perform one or two behaviors. When he performs the behavior you ask for, celebrate by acting goofy, running, throwing a toy for him to chase, letting him give you kisses, or playing tug-of-war. Be happy! Your dog will see that you are having a good time. Get him excited and then ask him to sit or to leave an object alone or to lie down and stay. Pause and wait. Once he performs the behavior, release him and celebrate again. The reward is play—food doesn't need to be part of this game. Play the game for short periods of time when your dog is bored, hyperactive, or needs exercise.

Summary

- Teaching your dog to stay happens gradually.

- Teach your dog to stay at different angles to him, including having your back to him.

- Teach your dog to sit or lie down in the settings that you want him to stay in before you begin teaching him to stay.

- Reward your dog for staying—not for breaking the stay.

- If your dog breaks a stay, first ask him to sit or lie down again before giving the instruction to stay. If he continues to break position, decrease the amount of time you ask him to stay for. You may also need to limit the distractions around him.

- Teach your dog a release word so that he knows when he is no longer expected to perform a behavior.

- To increase the distance between yourself and your dog as you are teaching him an instruction, you may leash him, keep him behind a baby gate, or have a friend stand next to him and give him treats for you. Stand next to your dog at first. Ask him to perform a behavior. Reward him when he performs it and then step away from him. Ask him to perform the behavior again. When he complies, return to him to reward him or let your friend give him a treat.

- Exaggerate your hand motions and speak louder when signaling to your dog from a distance.

- Reinforce all the behaviors that you teach your dog by playing the Crazy Human and Dog game. You can both have fun and act silly while your dog learns to listen to you.

Chapter Four

Other Behaviors

Calming Body Language

Humans tend to use intense body language when interacting with other animals. As primates, we reach in front of us to grab and touch objects and we face individuals directly. Direct frontal body language can frighten and inhibit many dogs. It can also intensify anxiety and aggression, increase mouthiness, and cause a dog to jump on you. By being cognizant of your body language and modifying it around dogs you can make them more relaxed and comfortable with you.

Angle yourself slightly when interacting with dogs, as opposed to facing them directly or leaning over them. Stand or kneel parallel or at a perpendicular angle to them. Pet your dog under his chin and on his chest. Try not to face him directly as you pet him.

Fig 27. Petting Kiva on her chest. My hand remains under her head.
©2007 Kerri Fenn

When he approaches, sniffs, or even kisses you, avert your gaze slightly for a moment. Your dog will find this a friendly gesture. If he gets too excited around you, turn your back on him and cease all eye contact. Only pay attention to him when he calms down.

Fig 28. Encouraging Jake to approach by orienting my body away from him slightly. This is friendly body language.
©2007 Lauren MacDonald

When introducing your dog to a new person, bend down and kneel next to him to keep him from jumping. This will also encourage other people to stand next to him or to approach him from the side. Give your dog treats while someone new is petting him on the head. When the new person stops petting your dog, stop giving him treats. Your dog is less likely to jump while he is eating and may come to enjoy being petted on the head.

How to Prevent and Resolve Jumping

Memorize this statement: "Life happens on all fours." Give your dog all the attention that he desires and deserves, but only do so when he has all four paws on the ground. Try to catch and reward these behaviors (i.e., standing, sitting, and lying down) before your dog feels it is in his best interests to jump. If he needs to show you that he is

Fig 29. *Turning my back to Kiva when she jumps.*
©2007 Kerri Fenn

sitting by jumping on you first to get your attention, you will end up reinforcing jumping—not sitting.

If your dog jumps on you, end all eye contact and pivot away from him. You may have to do this a few times before he calms down. When he is on all fours again, give him attention, eye contact, or whatever else it was that he wanted. If you have something that your dog wants and he jumps on you, remove the item or turn away from him. When he is on all fours again, offer him the item.

Use this same approach when sitting on sofas or chairs. The instant that your dog jumps on you, remove eye contact and pivot your legs away from him. Give him attention when he is back on all fours. Do not give him attention too quickly after he jumps. Wait at least three to five seconds before you interact with him again. If he climbs all over you while you are seated, stand up and turn your back to him. Withdraw all attention until he calms down.

Tips for Discouraging Jumping Up on Guests and for Meeting People Outside

Entryways: Direct your dog to an activity away from the door. Call him to you whenever a person enters and have him sit or lie down for food treats. Play with him with toys from a toy bin whenever someone enters the house. Teach him to fetch or play tug with a toy. Give him something to chew on or carry. Dogs tend not to jump when they are carrying objects in their mouths. Visitors should remain calm and not give your dog too much attention immediately upon entering. Likewise, stay relaxed when you open the door and greet guests.

Outside: If your dog really likes treats, you can teach him that whenever he meets a new person, if he sits, he will get a treat. You can also give him treats for sitting when a person approaches. If your dog jumps or stands up, the person can walk away from him and you can stop giving your dog treats. You can practice this exercise with a friend. Eventually your friend should be able to approach your dog and pet him while your dog remains calm and sits.

Teach your dog to walk with you and to look at you when people pass by. Give him treats when a person passes and stop when the person has passed. While talking to a stranger, reward your dog for standing, sitting, or lying down. You do not necessarily need to instruct him to sit, stand, or lie down; just give him treats whenever he exhibits these behaviors and he will perform them more often.

Chewing and Play-Biting

All puppies and young dogs mouth objects and play-bite in order to explore the environment. Just as human toddlers explore the environment by touching and tasting, young dogs and puppies want to chew the world—or at least try to taste it. When puppies and dogs are overly tired they may also act out. If you find that your dog is out of control and none of the methods below seem to help, he may just need a good nap.

Prevention is the best way to deal with chewing and play-biting. Give your dog a toy bin filled with fun toys. Keep food dispensing toys in a separate location. Always play with your dog with toys from the bin and keep it in an accessible location. Reward and praise your dog for getting toys from the toy bin. When your dog is done playing with his toys, put them back into the bin. Do not leave the toys on the floor or they will lose value for your dog. To prevent chewing, apply all-natural concentrated citrus sprays onto items that you do not want damaged. Most dogs do not like the smell of citrus and will avoid objects that have been sprayed. Never use synthetic chemical sprays.

The following exercises should help to eliminate play-biting and will teach your dog to bite or mouth you softly. If you try to eliminate play-biting too soon—especially in young puppies—two things may happen: One, you fail miserably and unintentionally encourage your dog to mouth or bite you harder. Two, you succeed, and your dog never learns to control how hard he bites.

Dogs who live in groups have good mouth control. They play, give each other kisses, and crush bone by varying the amount of pressure that they exert with their mouths and jaws. Mouth control is a learned behavior. A young puppy develops mouth control by playing with other dogs. When dogs play, if one dog bites too hard, the dog who gets bitten immediately stops playing.

Your puppy will instinctively learn to inhibit his bite if you stop playing and interacting with him the instant he bites or mouths you too hard. If you try to reprimand or punish him by yelling at him, grabbing his muzzle, or pinning him to the ground, you will just get him more excited and encourage him to continue to attack you or frighten him so badly that he doesn't want to play with you anymore. Neither method will teach him mouth control.

Teaching Dogs to Soften Their Mouths and Eliminate Play-Biting

If your dog bites really hard during play, begin this exercise when his bite hurts you or when you can feel his teeth. If your dog is older but still bites hard, begin this exercise as soon as you can feel pressure. When it seems like your dog is becoming sensitive to how hard he is biting you, you can implement this exercise at times when he mouths you or bites you softly even when it doesn't hurt. Teach your dog that humans are wimps when it comes to being bitten.

When your dog bites you, make a quick high-pitched noise to startle him. This "ouch" cue should sound like a yelp—not a scolding or a punishment. But don't keep whimpering incessantly; your dog will just think that you're weird. As soon as he bites you, make your yelping noise and stop making eye contact. If your dog looks startled or perplexed and tries to solicit your attention, ignore him. You are giving him a time-out for hurting you. Do not interact with him. Do not say "No." Do not take him into another room. Ignore him for about 20 seconds. This teaches him that it hurts you when he bites you and that if he bites you, you won't play with him anymore. He should be able to associate your "ouch" noise with the bite. Timing is important. If you yelp when he hasn't bitten you, he won't understand why you are telling him that you're hurt.

After about 20 seconds, play with your dog again. You want to let him know that even though you like him and want to play, you don't like it when he bites you. If he mouths or bites you softly, you may allow it. You can always redirect the behavior and encourage your dog to play with a toy. After a time out, if your dog continues to bite you and it hurts, yelp the instant he bites and ignore him again. Do not make eye contact with him. This time ignore him for about 40 seconds. Under no circumstances should you interact with him.

After the second time out, play with your dog again. Encourage him to play with his toys or pet him gently while sitting next to him. If he bites you again, yelp or give your "ouch" cue and leave the room. Do not bring him with you and be sure that he can't follow you. It is more effective if you leave him alone for the time-out. After about 60 seconds, play with him again. Always encourage him to play with his toys.

If your dog bites your clothing or legs as you walk, freeze. Most puppies grow out of this, and if you react, you will encourage him to keep attacking you. Be boring. Don't move. If your dog is obsessed with your clothing or biting your legs, spray a little citrus spray on your clothing. This should keep him from wanting to bite you further. Only yelp or make an "ouch" noise when he touches your skin. If you need to physically remove him from your pant leg, be very calm and avoid making eye contact with him while doing so. Again, most dogs grow out of this behavior. Administer a time-out and leave the room if you have to, but do not interact with him and encourage the behavior.

The Importance and Value of a Toy Bin

Toy bins are wonderful for dogs—even for dogs who are unsure of how to play. Dogs love to hoard, and it is important to teach them what is theirs and what isn't. There are surely many items in your home that you don't want your dog to chew, including children's toys. Likewise, there are toys and stuffed animals that you do want your dog to play with. He will not know which toys are for him unless you teach him.

There are other benefits to having a toy bin. If an object stays on the floor and nobody wants it or uses it, it loses its value for your dog. If a guest comes over and you want to redirect your dog to a toy or encourage him to play, he will have no interest in playing with a toy that has been left untouched on the floor. By keeping his toys in a bin, you will not only increase their value, but also be able to direct him to his bin to play with his toys when you want to teach him not to jump on your friends or chew on your sofa.

Fig 30. Lucy chooses a toy from the toy bin.
©2007 Margaret Crow

Keep your dog's toys in a large, shallow bin—a plastic storage box works well. Your dog should be able to choose the toys he likes from his bin. If the bin is too deep he might not be able to find his favorite toys. When your dog is finished playing with toys you should put them back in the bin. Rotate your dog's toy selection every few weeks or whenever he loses interest in them. After a few weeks, you can act as if old toys are new, and your dog will likely be interested in them again. This makes toys last longer and saves you money. Occasionally put cookies in the bin. If your dog is chewing your sofa or chasing you or wanting to play in a way that you find unacceptable, redirect him to his toy bin and praise him every time he gets a toy from his bin. You want him to play with his toys, so make a fuss and give him lots of attention when he does!

Summary

- Memorize the statement "Life happens on all fours." Give your dog all the attention that he desires and deserves but only when he has all four paws on the ground.

- The instant your dog jumps on you stop making eye contact and pivot away from him. Do so even when seated.

- Be calm when you open the door to greet guests. Redirect your dog to an activity away from the door if you don't want him jumping on guests and visitors.

- Your dog will jump less when he has something in his mouth.

- Teach your dog that the presence or arrival of strangers and guests results in getting food treats and attention when he sits or lies down.

- While speaking with another person, give your dog treats for standing, sitting, or lying down to reinforce and reward appropriate, calm behavior.

- All puppies and young dogs naturally want to mouth and play-bite. They want to explore their environments with their mouths. Fill a bin with toys and use it to teach your dog what is appropriate for him to chew on. Redirect your dog to his toys when he chews on something that you don't want him to chew on.

- Spray all-natural concentrated orange spray on anything that you do not want your dog to chew. Never use synthetic chemical sprays.

- To eliminate play-biting and soften your dog's bite, yelp the instant he bites you too hard and give him a brief time-out. Stop making eye contact or leave the room.

- If you try to eliminate play-biting too soon, especially in puppies under 3 months of age, you may fail to teach them how to bite softly.

- If your dog bites at your clothing or legs, stop moving. Be boring. Most young dogs grow out of this behavior.

Barking and Teaching Quiet

If your dog seems to bark continuously, try to figure out why. Is he afraid? Does he want treats or your attention? Is he happy, lonely, or anxious? The key to solving barking problems is to understand why your dog is barking.

Attention-Seeking Barking (Barking to interact with you or to get something from you.)

Increase your dog's exercise. A tired dog is a relaxed dog, and a relaxed dog barks less. A long morning walk or run or an hour of interactive play will release some of your dog's pent-up energy and frustration. This will make it easier for you to give him attention when he is quiet and not barking.

Instruct your dog to lie down or redirect him to an activity that is incompatible with barking. Try to anticipate his barks and redirect his attention or ask him to perform a behavior that is incompatible with barking before he starts. Make these alternate behaviors rewarding for him.

Give your dog treat-dispensing toys to keep him busy during the day and when you are not home. If he is physically and mentally stimulated, he will be less anxious and bark less. The TwistnTreat and The Groove Thing, both by Premier, are two good starter toys for most dogs. Treat-dispensing toys should be washed out regularly to prevent mold.

Only give your dog attention or make eye contact with him when he is *not* barking, and be careful not to reward him for anything too soon after a bark; you could end up reinforcing the barking.

Try reverse psychology. The instant your dog barks, offer him something that he has no interest in.

Leave the room and give your dog a time-out when he barks. The best way to give a time-out is to cue it. Give your dog one warning as soon as he barks. He will have no idea what your warning means and will continue to bark at you. Then immediately cue his time-out by saying "That's it," "Done," or "I'm outta here," and leave the room. Time-outs should last no more than a few minutes.

Barking in the House out of Boredom

Increase your dog's exercise and play interactive games with him. Feed him meals with treat-dispensing toys.

If your dog is barking at something outside, close the blinds or shades immediately when he starts.

Redirect your dog by giving him all-natural, unsalted peanut butter before he starts barking or right after he begins. He will lick the roof of his mouth instead of barking. You can also do this when he barks at you for attention. Just make sure you don't give him peanut butter every time he barks at you, or he might start barking at you for peanut butter.

Acknowledge the bark. Look at what your dog is barking at and then direct him away from the source of the bark and reward him for doing something that is incompatible with barking, such as chewing on or playing with a toy, lying down, or being brushed.

Barking at Others out of Fear or While Outside on the Leash

Pair highly desirable treats with whatever it is that your dog finds frightening. Feed him in the presence of whatever it is that scares him. Be relaxed. Keep him at a distance from the threat so that he feels less anxious. If he is afraid of strangers, ask other people to ignore him. They can casually toss him treats, but should not try to interact with or pet him.

Give your dog treats for paying attention to you and looking at you. Reinforce any and all eye contact he gives you.

Teach your dog to perform other behaviors, such as lying down, looking at you, walking next to you, or sitting when he is in the presence of something that makes him anxious.

Reward your dog when he does not bark.

Summary

- The key to resolving barking issues is figuring out why your dog is barking.

- A tired dog will be relaxed and bark less.

- Give your dog attention when he is not barking. If he barks at you continually, more than likely you have been reinforcing his barking.

- Try to anticipate a bark and redirect your dog to an activity that is incompatible with barking.

- If your dog is barking because he is scared, pair especially good treats with whatever it is that he finds scary. Reward him for performing other behaviors, such as looking at you and walking with you.

- Reward your dog when he is quiet. Do not encourage barking by reacting to him when he barks. Don't yell at him—especially if he wants your attention.

Housetraining

Housetraining a dog—whether a puppy or an older dog—takes patience. Dogs cannot be housetrained overnight, however much we might want to see this happen. Fortunately, dogs can be housetrained within a few weeks or months—as opposed to human children, who usually take a couple of years. But the principles of toilet-training children and housetraining dogs are very similar.

Never punish your dog for peeing or pooping—regardless of the location. Punishment will only scare him, and he will become afraid of urinating or defecating in front of you. If he will not eliminate in front of you, it will be difficult for you to reward him for going in the right location.

Housetraining can be summarized in three steps: Set your dog up for success by establishing a location in which you would like him to eliminate. Make it rewarding for him to pee or poop in that location. Ensure that he never has an opportunity to eliminate in an undesirable location by supervising him and managing his environment.

Housetraining Principles

When you are not able to supervise your dog directly he should be confined to an area small enough that he will not want to urinate or defecate there. Dogs do not want to pee or poop where they eat or sleep or in any other personal spaces or living areas. You can gate off part of a room or use an ex-pen, which is a playpen made for dogs. Make sure this area is comfortable for your dog and has a soft surface or dog bed for him to lie down on.

Since dogs prefer not to go to the bathroom in their living areas, your dog must have access to the areas in your home where you would like him to be housetrained. You can tether him to you when you are at home by hooking a leash to your waist. This way he can follow you when you change rooms and will have access to all the rooms of the house where you want him to be. You will be able to see the signs that may indicate that he has to go to the bathroom, such as pacing, randomly sniffing, whimpering, looking at you, play-biting you, or squatting. If you spend most of your time in one room, gate off that room so that your dog doesn't have access to other areas of the house. Whenever your dog pees or poops in a certain location, he learns from that experience and may come to prefer pottying there—especially if you don't remove the odors.

Instead of randomly taking your dog to the place that you have chosen for him to go to the bathroom, take him at times that he is likely to have to go. Most dogs tend to urinate 10-30 minutes after they drink and defecate 10-40 minutes after they eat. Young puppies, however, will not be able to hold it this long. All dogs tend to pee or poop immediately upon waking (even from a quick nap); after play and exercise; during or immediately following anxious, exciting, or stressful situations such a visit from a friend; and before going to sleep at night.

Teach your dog a word that indicates the location—either outside or on a pee pad—in which you would like him to go to the bathroom. Say the word in an upbeat tone just before or while you are taking him to that location.

Also teach your dog words for urinating and defecating. Cue words can be "potty," "park it," "hurry up," "pee-pee," or "poo-poo." You get the idea! While your dog is peeing or pooping, say the words you have chosen. He should eventually know to eliminate upon hearing your words.

Give your dog an especially good food treat after he pees or poops in your desired location. Dogs do not know the value of hardwood floors or oriental rugs. Without training, your dog has no real motivation to wait to relieve himself. Urinating and defecating feel good to him, and delaying elimination is uncomfortable and ultimately unhealthy. By giving your dog an especially good food treat after eliminating, you are increasing his motivation to go outside, on a pad, or in a litter box.

Give your dog a lot of praise when he urinates or defecates in the proper location.

When taking your dog outside to eliminate, linger in one area. Do not go for a walk or keep changing locations. It will be easier for him to learn to go to the bathroom in a specific area if you keep taking him to the same general location.

Take your dog for walks *after* he urinates or defecates. Walking and playing with you can be used as rewards. If you routinely end a walk or take your dog inside after he pees or poops, he may learn to hold it so that he can stay outdoors or keep walking.

Never punish or reprimand your dog for urinating or defecating. He will begin peeing or pooping when you are not looking because he will become afraid to urinate or defecate in front of you.

Your dog will need a way to let you know that he has to potty—especially if he is expected to eliminate outside. Teach him a way to let you know when he needs to go. It is up to you to pay attention to his signals.

Signals and Using a Bell

Some common behaviors that may indicate that your dog needs to eliminate include walking in circles, wandering, standing or walking by the door, looking at the door, mouthing you, barking at you, or staring at you. If your dog looks perplexed or seems to be trying to find something to do, more than likely he needs to pee or poop!

If your dog isn't housetrained, it is best to assume that any unfocused behavior is a sign that he needs to pee or poop. Even if you're occasionally wrong, every time that you are right you will encourage your dog to go to the bathroom where you want him to.

Teach your dog to ring a bell. Most dogs can learn to do this fairly easily. This is a nice way for your dog to let others know that he wants to be let outside. Hang a bell on the doorknob of the door that you use to take your dog outside. Sleigh bells or "jingle bells" work well. The bells will ring every time the door opens, and your dog will learn to associate the sound of the bells with the door. Be sure that he can reach at least one bell; he will need to be able to nudge it.

Most dogs do this with their muzzles. Show your dog the bell before you take him outside. Ring it, say "outside" (or whatever word you have chosen to designate the area in which he goes to the bathroom), and open the door. At some point your dog will ring the bell on his own. The instant he does, celebrate! Say your word and immediately take him outside.

Your dog will not automatically understand that he is supposed to ring the bell if he needs to eliminate. The first time he rings the bell, you will probably be thrilled. Consequently, your dog may ring the bell to get your attention. He may want to go outside to play and not necessarily have to pee or poop. If you have a fenced-in location where he can run freely, this arrangement may work for you. Regardless of why he rings the bell, however, you must take him outside when he does so. If you take him outside and he does not have to go to the bathroom, take him back inside and make sure that he doesn't go somewhere you don't want him to. Then, try again.

If your dog gets into the habit of ringing the bell to get your attention, do not automatically assume he does not need to potty when he rings the bell. If you ignore him, it will likely turn out that he really did need to pee or poop, and you will have a big mess to clean up.

Put your dog on a consistent feeding schedule. Do not leave him a bowl of food to nibble. If you do not know how much or how often he is eating, you will have trouble predicting when he has to go to the bathroom. Whether you feed him snacks throughout the day or only feed him at mealtimes, you must be aware of when and how much he has eaten. It is not fair to your dog if he is relying on you to take him outside and you do not know when he needs to eliminate.

If your dog eliminates in an inappropriate location use a cleaner containing enzymes specifically designed to eliminate odors. Products such as Anti-Icky Poo, Simple Solution, and Petastic work well.

If you catch your dog pottying in an area that you don't want him to, get his attention *before* he finishes, say your word for the location in which you want him to go, and rush him to the place you have chosen. Then praise him and give him treats for peeing or pooping in the correct location.

Summary

- The principles of house-training can be summarized in three steps: Manage your dog's environment so that he is unable to potty where you do not want him to; give your dog many opportunities to eliminate in the location that you have chosen; and make it rewarding for him to eliminate there.

- Teach your dog a word for the location that you have chosen and words for peeing and pooping.

- Give your dog a highly desirable treat immediately after he eliminates in the location that you have chosen.

- Do not punish your dog for eliminating in a location that you don't want him to.

- Use odor-eliminators containing enzymes on areas of the carpet and floor that your dog has soiled.

- Keep in mind that dogs tend to urinate or defecate immediately upon waking from naps, after drinking and eating, when stressed or excited, during and following exercise and play, and before going to sleep at night.

- Teach your dog to ring a bell so that he can signal to you that he needs to be let outside.

Stool-Eating (Coprophagia)

Some dogs and puppies will eat their own or another dog's stools. There are different theories as to why some dogs do this, but, to my knowledge, there are no definite conclusions. This is sometimes a problem with small dogs as they are being pad-trained. Some dogs will simply outgrow it. Many taste-aversive products don't seem to be very effective, and so you might want to try several of the following strategies.

Dogs who eat stools may be lacking something in their diets. Often this is raw food that contains cellulose and fiber (i.e., plant roughage). Packaged food does not have a lot of the life-giving energy that animals need. Often dogs who eat poop also eat a lot of grass, shove sticks or rocks in their mouths, and eat dirt, sometimes to a frenetic level. If your dog is exhibiting any of these behaviors, make his diet more holistic and nutritious by adding roughage and fiber. Any kind of plant food, such as brown rice, carrots, a spoonful of canned pumpkin or pineapple, spinach, and other vegetables, will do. You can also add papain digestive enzyme capsules to your dog's food.

Stool-eating is sometimes a learned behavior, and therefore it can become a habit. The less frequently your dog exhibits this behavior, the less likely it is that the behavior will continue. Teach your dog alternate behaviors to perform after he or another dog defecates. You can teach him to come to you and sit for a food treat after he or another dog poops, or you can teach him to "Leave it" by using an interruption such as "Ah-Ah" or "Hey" and then rewarding him for backing away from the poop.

By all means, try taste-aversive products. As far as I know, they are safe. Just don't be too disheartened if they don't seem to work. If they do, celebrate! Forbid and meat tenderizer are popular taste aversives.

Always try to pick up stools before your dog has a chance to eat them. If you catch him eating his feces, interrupt or distract him and ask him to exhibit another behavior.

Chapter Five

Behavior Modification for Fear, Aggression, and Anxiety

Prevent and Manage

When you are not able to actively work on alleviating your dog's fears or anxieties, try not to expose him to whatever it is that makes him nervous. If you expose him to things that frighten him or make him anxious you will simply reinforce fearful or anxious behavior. If he becomes fearful in specific situations and you let these situations continue to occur, you will not be doing anything to improve his physical, mental, or emotional state.

Fearful and aggressive dogs need help. You should never reprimand or scold your dog when he is frightened or nervous. Growling, snarling, crying, panting, and whining are emotional reactions. These behaviors may annoy you, but reprimanding your dog for exhibiting them will not address the source of the problem. Always try to be as gentle and positive with your dog as you can be. He can conquer his fears—but only with your help.

An aggressive dog requires more management. You must prevent the events that trigger your dog's aggression, and you need to protect him and other people, dogs, and animals from injury. Aggression stems from stress and anxiety. Once you find out why your dog is stressed and anxious, you will be better able to rectify his aggression. Work with a positive trainer on any aggression issue that makes you uncomfortable. Trying to figure it out on your own can be problematic for both you and your dog.

How to Help a Fearful or Aggressive Dog

Desensitize your dog to whatever it is that causes him stress. Expose him gradually to things that make him nervous, but do so at a pace or a level that doesn't cause him to get upset or become reactive. If your dog seems upset or stressed in any way when exposed to triggers that previously caused him stress, you are not desensitizing him.

Counter-condition your dog to what makes him nervous by changing his associations with his stressors. You can do this by pairing things that he loves with things that he dislikes. When you expose your dog to a low-level stressor (desensitization), pair it with something he adores, such as food, baby talk, walks, play, toys, or gentle touch. The positive experience that you provide for him should be more potent than the stressor he is being exposed to. The goal is to lead him to enjoy what he initially disliked. This is not bribery. You are changing your dog's perception of what previously made him nervous.

You will need to provide your dog with highly desirable food or treats when working through his fears. Use whole food instead of processed dog snacks. Sometimes dogs like carob and molasses treats. Dogs also tend to prefer soft foods over crunchy. Every dog has certain preferences. If your dog has a medical condition or requires a special diet, please meet with your veterinarian to see if there is something that you can give him that will allow you to implement behavior modification techniques at home.

Do not get angry or tense if your dog growls. Be positive and calm. Redirect him from the negative experience to a behavior that is rewarding for you both. Avoid stressful situations that cause him to growl or become upset by managing his environment so that these situations do not repeatedly occur.

Watch your body language. Never approach or confront a fearful dog. A dog who is afraid of a person or another dog should always be the one to approach or initiate interactions. A fearful dog should never be directly confronted with what frightens him.

Always position yourself at an angle to fearful dogs. Stand or kneel parallel or at a perpendicular angle to dogs. Facing dogs and staring at them can make them frightened or anxious. Petting your dog directly on the head can be threatening and may make him uncomfortable. Pet him under his chin or on his chest and approach him from the side. Angle your body away from him as you pet him, especially if he is fearful.

Fig 31. Calming body language. This position is great for dogs who do not want to approach on leash or for dogs who are timid. ©2007 Lauren MacDonald

Fig 32. Orienting my body away from Bessie and Jake cause them to look at me and orient in my direction. ©2007 Lauren MacDonald

Direct eye contact unnerves dogs. Never stare down a dog. It will not establish your dominance, and you will scare or intimidate him. Your dog will appreciate it if you look away at times or look at him without staring.

Never jerk your dog with the leash. Leash jerks can cause tension and fear and will just make your dog more reactive.

If you get stressed when you are out with your dog, walk or run with an iPod and listen to your favorite music. You will remain calm and not put off so much nervous energy. This may help your dog relax, and he will find it easier to pay attention to you.

If your dog is fearful or nervous around strangers, pair people with positive experiences for him. People can give your dog treats when he approaches them or can toss them to him. If he is overly nervous or anxious around strangers, ask them to ignore him. You may need to be the one to give him treats if accepting food directly from strangers is too scary for him.

Knowing how to get and maintain your dog's attention and eye contact, teaching him good recall skills, and learning how to hold the leash properly (so it stays relaxed around his neck) can all help if your dog is fearful or aggressive.

Harnesses such as the Sense-ation Sensible or Easy-Walk are good to have when working with fearful or aggressive dogs. A Gentle Leader can be useful when managing aggressive dogs who may have a tendency to bite people or other animals. Attention exercises can help counter-condition your dog to eye contact if eye contact makes him nervous or uncomfortable (see p. 13).

Products such as Comfort Zone (Dog Appeasing Pheromone), melatonin, and/or pharmaceutical medication may help to alleviate your dog's anxiety. Speak with your veterinarian if you are interested in pharmacological intervention.

If your dog gets nervous when you have company over, designate a place where he can go to feel safe. This place should have a positive association for him and no one should intrude on him while he is there.

Learn leash techniques so that you can position your dog in ways that are more comfortable for him when outside in stressful situations.

These four techniques can help his fearful or aggressive behavior:

- Position yourself between your dog and the stressor.

Fig 33. Keeping yourself between your dog and another dog can prevent your dog from becoming too aroused or distracted.
©2007 Margaret Crow

- Walk in a semi-circle around the stressor, increasing the distance between your dog and the stressor.

- Position your dog so that his back is to the stressor. This is especially important if the stressor is close by.

Fig 34. Positioning your dog's back to another dog can help keep your dog calm and attentive to you.
©2007 Margaret Crow

- Make a U-turn and walk in the opposite direction of the stressor. Do not force your dog to experience something that he can't handle.

Do not use choke, pinch, or shock collars when working with a fearful or aggressive dog. Harsh training techniques will intensify your dog's fearfulness and aggression.

Purchase *On Talking Terms With Dogs* by Turid Rugaas, which has many pictures that will help you read your dog's body language. Another book, *Canine Body Language: A photographic Guide Interpreting the Native Language of the Domestic Dog* by Brenda Aloff is also a good choice. These books can make working with a fearful or aggressive dog easier for you.

There are several stages to working with fearful and aggressive dogs and applying desensitization and counter-conditioning techniques. These stages may overlap.

The first stage consists of pairing experiences your dog loves with whatever it is that scares or frightens him. If he is too fearful or reactive or will not accept the treats that you provide, he is overwhelmed: You are exposing him to more than he can handle or the treats you are offering are not especially desirable. If you are applying desensitization and counter-conditioning techniques correctly, your dog will come to associate the treats that you provide with the experience that previously stressed him and will begin to look forward to that experience.

Once your dog anticipates getting treats during a stressful situation, he will make eye contact with you and may appear calmer or happier around the stressor. Then you can proceed to the second stage. Begin giving your dog copious treats for performing nonreactive behaviors, such as paying attention to you; being relaxed, calm, or happy; or sitting or lying down. He should not be as fearful or anxious as he used to be.

Then you can move to the third stage and begin to reinforce behaviors such as sitting, being in a "down" position, staying, and coming when called. Your dog should be able to look to you for guidance and feel comfortable around his previous stressor. He will want to be able to do something to earn rewards. At this stage, you can teach him what you would like him to do when a stressor is present. Do you want him to look at you when other dogs pass? Would you like him to sit at the curb while cars pass or give you a high five and make eye contact? Do you want him to lie down next to you when a guest comes over or to go to his safe area in another room?

During the final stage of this process you can begin to expose your dog to a group environment if he was fearful of other dogs or people. A positive group class or Feisty Fido class can be helpful at this point.

Summary

- If you are not able to work on alleviating your dog's fears, don't expose him to whatever it is that makes him nervous.

- Fearful and aggressive dogs need help. Dogs should never be reprimanded or scolded when they are frightened.

- Aggressive dogs require more management. Protect your dog from exposure to his stressor, and keep him, other dogs or animals, and other people from getting hurt.

- Do not get angry or tense if your dog growls, but be positive and calm, and direct him away from the negative experience.

- Desensitize and counter-condition your dog to those things that make him anxious or upset.

- You will need to give your dog highly desirable treats as you are working through his fears.

- Watch your body language around fearful dogs. Always position yourself at an angle to a fearful dog.

- Direct eye contact and staring unnerves dogs. Never stare down dogs.

- Reward your dog for making eye contact by doing the attention exercise (see p. 13). This can be helpful if he is afraid to make eye contact with you or becomes fearful when people look at him.

- A head halter can help manage your dog so that he cannot bite someone. A front-clip harness can help prevent him from lunging or pulling on the leash.

- Never jerk on the leash or use pinch, shock, or choke collars.

- If your dog is scared of strangers, designate a place where he can go to feel safe when you have company over.

- Learn proper leash techniques so that you can position your dog in a way that is more comfortable for him when he is exposed to a stressful situation.

- Get the support of a professional behaviorist, trainer, or consultant for help resolving your dog's fear or aggression issues.

Separation Anxiety

Apply the principles of desensitization and counter-conditioning to prevent your dog from becoming anxious when someone he is attached to leaves or he is left alone. Pair your absence with something positive that will keep your dog busy for most, if not all, of the time that you are gone. When you reappear, remove the treats you gave him when you left. You want your dog to want you to leave the house.

Your dog should not be left alone unless you are able to pair a positive experience with your absence. You may have to hire a pet sitter, ask a friend to watch your dog while you are away, or take your dog to a doggie-daycare facility or playgroup. If your dog is the only animal in the household, adding a second dog to the family may help.

Expose your dog to the experience of being left alone for only short periods of time. If he becomes nervous, anxious, or fearful before you leave, pair positive experiences with "cues" for your departure, such as having a cup of coffee or putting on a sweater. The instant you cue your departure, give your dog a highly desirable treat. He should be occupied by the treat most, if not all, of the time it takes you to have a cup of coffee or put on your sweater.

Some other techniques that may help remedy separation anxiety include teaching your dog how to play interactive games, such as "finding" games and scavenger hunts. These games can keep him entertained while you are gone. Give him toys that dispense treats when you leave the house.

Do not ignore your dog when you return, but do not be too excited, either. Also, if you are upset when you leave, he will be even more upset than usual when he's alone.

Try increasing your dog's exercise. If you can exercise him before you leave, he will probably take a nap when you are gone. Morning hikes, running, biking, and playing with other dogs at dog parks are good forms of exercise.

Leave your dog in a comfortable location. Do not put him in a crate to resolve separation anxiety. Putting him in a crate to prevent damage to your property will not resolve his fear or anxiety issues and can, in fact, make his anxiety worse.

If you do come home and find things damaged, do not reprimand or punish your dog. This will only contribute to his anxiety.

Spend time positively training your dog. Positive training gives dogs confidence, enhances their ability to communicate with you, and keeps them stimulated.

Country and classical music may also help dogs relax.

If your dog's separation anxiety is severe, medication may be helpful. Please speak with your veterinarian.

Professional help is valuable when resolving any behavioral problem. Please see a professional animal behavior consultant or behaviorist if you have a dog with severe separation anxiety.

Preparation for Thunderstorms and Fireworks

Here are several tips to ease your dog's anxiety during or before a storm or when fireworks are scheduled:

Use reverse psychology. Try to make thunderstorms and fireworks relaxing and positive for your dog. Don't act as if something is wrong or continuously try to soothe him; this will just validate his fears. Try to pair these experiences with things that your dog really loves. Be gentle and positive. Stay relaxed.

Teach your dog to go to a location where you know he feels comfortable. Choose a place away from any windows or the outer walls of the house so that sounds are muffled and he does not have to hear the windows rattle.

If your dog will eat, give him treats continuously during fireworks and storms. Pick treats that really make his mouth water. He may be too nervous to eat at first, but if the food is highly desirable he might end up trying it.

Install a Comfort Zone diffuser in the area your dog will be in during storms or fireworks.

Muffle noise by closing blinds, curtains, and windows. Place jumbo cotton balls in your dog's ears. Be careful not to place the cotton balls too far into his ear canals, and don't forget to remove them when the storm is over!

Feed your dog a carbohydrate-rich meal before a storm. Mashed potatoes, pasta, and overcooked rice may help him relax and make him feel sleepy.

If you want to comfort your dog, by all means, stay with him—but remember to appear calm and happy. Try not to be overly consoling; this will simply reinforce his anxiety.

Special capes designed for dogs who are frightened during storms are available online from www.stormdefender.com. Although they look a little bit goofy, the capes help some dogs calm down. Why they work is unclear; dogs may find the weight of the capes soothing, or the capes may protect them from static electricity. Anxiety wraps may also help dogs to relax. They are sold online from www.anxietywrap.com.

Car Sickness

Many dogs get car-sick. After one or two bad experiences, your dog may get anxious just looking at a car. You can try spraying Comfort Zone in the car to relax him.

Expose your dog to the car slowly. Pair the exposure with something positive. Stop exposing him to the car before he becomes stressed or upset. This may mean giving him treats as you approach the car. When you turn around and walk away from the car, stop giving him treats.

You can also try giving him treats as he gets into the car or as you start the engine. When you turn the engine off or when your dog gets out of the car, stop giving him treats. You may want to begin by simply spending time with him in the car. Give him treats and play with him and keep the engine off. Then go for a brief walk. This may be a day's training. Expose your dog to the car gradually, until he feels comfortable taking short car rides.

Keep the windows of your car partially open to allow fresh air to circulate or keep the air conditioner running. Defrost or heat from the car can intensify your dog's queasy feeling.

Take your dog for short car rides to fun places. If your dog goes to the vet or the groomer every time he's in the car, he will learn to associate car rides with unpleasant experiences.

Sometimes being in a crate can intensify car-sickness for dogs. Use a dog seatbelt instead of a crate and/or keep your dog toward the front of the car to prevent nausea.

Cocculus is a good homeopathic remedy for car-sickness and can be found in many natural food stores. Dramamine will not cure car-sickness and may cause drowsiness.

Pull over if your dog gets ill. Take him for a brief walk and give him some fresh air.

Take your dog for walks before and after riding in the car. Do not feed him before car rides.

Chapter Six

Walking on a Leash

Tools to Help with Walking

I recommend taking lessons with a positive trainer who can help you teach your dog not to pull on the leash. The right tools can also make it easier to walk a dog who pulls on the leash.

A Sof-touch leash has a bit of elastic at the end. Dogs feel tension in the elastic when they get to the end of the leash. This piece of elastic can prevent a sudden jerk on your dog's neck if you abruptly change direction. Sof-touch leashes are available at www.webtrail.com/petbehavior.

A Sense-ation Harness (available at www.softouchconcepts.com) or an Easy-Walk Harness by Premier Pet Products (available in most pet supply stores) both work on the same principle. The leash attaches to the front of the harness, which will lead your dog to rotate back in your direction if he pulls too far forward. These are humane tools and most dogs take to them easily. The harnesses are easy to put on and take off. They also help you get your dog's attention. Sometimes they can cause chafing—especially with dogs who have little to no hair under their forelegs or who are unaccustomed to wearing harnesses. If the Sense-ation Sensible or Easy Walk harness chafes your dog, a Halti, a Gentle Leader, a Sof-touch leash, a martingale-style collar, or another body harness style are also worth trying.

A Gentle Leader or Halti (both available in most pet supply stores) can be helpful in managing an aggressive dog. When your dog wears a Gentle Leader, you have more control over his muzzle and can prevent him from biting another person or another dog or animal. You can also interrupt his barking. Make sure to accustom your dog to wearing a Gentle Leader or a Halti before you use one. This can take a few weeks. In addition, make sure to learn proper leash techniques when using a Gentle Leader. Always keep the leash relaxed where it connects to the leader, and never jerk on a head halter.

Ultimately, rewarding your dog for not pulling on the leash and for walking with you are the best ways to teach him to stop pulling. Learning how to hold a leash properly so that you do not jerk on his neck is crucial. You can learn proper leash techniques by working with a positive trainer.

How to Hold a Leash Properly

How you hold the leash is very important when working with a dog who pulls or who is fearful, timid, or aggressive. Holding the leash correctly helps you control your dog, prevents you from jerking and yanking on his neck, and frees one of your hands so that you can give him treats or carry something he values on the walk. Basic leash techniques will give you more control over your dog's movements and give him a little bit more freedom at the same time.

Fig LC. Leash control.
©2007 Margaret Crow

The Basics

Let the loop or handle of the leash drape over your thumb. This will not only free up the fingers on that hand, but will also—with proper body alignment and mechanics—leave you with more strength if your dog lunges and pulls. Secure the leash with your fingers.

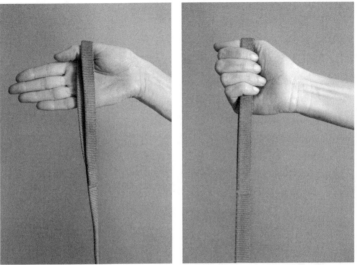

Fig. 35-36. How to hold a leash.
©2007 Margaret Crow

Keep your arms close to your body when your dog lunges. It is useless to use only your upper body strength to pull your dog when he lunges with all of his weight. If you do, you will have little choice but to yank back on your dog, which will not only reinforce his behavior but may result in muscle strain in your back and shoulders. If you freeze and tense your muscles, keeping your arms pinned close to your body, your dog will have to pull against your entire body weight. In addition, by not yanking back on your dog, you will encourage him not to pull you.

Always keep your wrist and forearm in line with your dog and at the same angle as the leash.

Because both of your hands are free when you hold the leash on your thumb, you can shorten the leash and stay in control of your dog while holding treats, a tennis ball, your car keys, or a clicker.

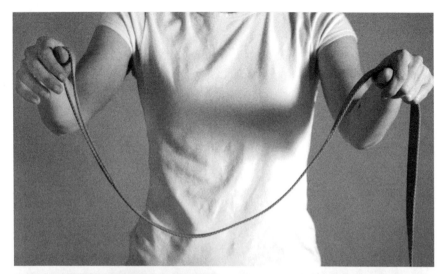

To shorten the leash, decide how much leash you would like to take and use the hand that isn't holding the leash to loop it around the thumb of the hand that is holding the leash. Always secure the leash by wrapping your fingers around the excess looped on your thumb. This will prevent the leash from slipping out of your hand and take the pressure off your thumb.

Fig. 37-40. How to shorten a leash.
©2007 Margaret Crow

You can shorten the leash without pulling your dog. If he pulls, walk toward him while you shorten the leash; you can also shorten it as he approaches you. Even though you may walk toward your dog, you do not have to let him continue to pull you. You can give your dog very little leash and still keep it relaxed around his neck. A relaxed leash simply means that there is no tension on the leash where it attaches to your dog's collar or harness.

Fig 41. A relaxed leash
©2007 Margaret Crow

You probably tend to lean forward or try to reel your dog in when he lunges or pulls against you. This not only puts you off balance, but keeps both of your hands on the leash, leaving neither available to give your dog treats for performing behaviors that you like.

There are two ways that you can stand to maintain your balance while your dog is pulling or lunging. One way is to turn toward the leash so that the length of the leash is in front of you and the side of your body faces your dog. By positioning yourself so that your side faces your dog, you will have more strength without needing to pull him. You will be able to keep him from pulling you or pursuing whatever he is lunging at.

Fig 42. Standing sideways to Kiva as she is pulling. This prevents me from unintentionally jerking her or moving forward.
©2007 Kerri Fenn

You can also position yourself with one leg in front of the other and lean back on your back leg as if you are going to sit down on a chair. You will have more strength because you will be employing the use of your legs and lower body—not your upper body or forearms.

Fig 43. Resting my weight on my back leg prevents me from leaning forward as Kiva tries to pull me.
©2007 Kerri Fenn

Please seek a professional qualified behaviorist, behavior consultant, or dog trainer to help you learn proper leash-holding techniques.

Walking With a Relaxed Leash

There are three techniques to use when teaching a dog to walk with you on a leash. They take some practice, but once you feel comfortable with the techniques your dog will begin to pay attention and you will both have more fun walking together.

Fig 44. A great way to feed a dog while walking. Use your open palm!
©2007 Kerri Fenn

As previously mentioned, dogs have an oppositional reflex. If you push or pull one way on your dog, he will push or pull instinctively in the opposite direction. The moment he feels tension on the leash he will naturally want to override it. He will pull against the tension, and in doing so he will pull against you. The more tension he feels, the more he will pull. If you continuously pull against him and he succeeds in going in his direction, he will learn that when he feels resistance on the leash he just has to pull harder to go where he wants to.

It is important to teach your dog from the beginning that pulling on you does not make you move forward. This means that you can't pull back on him. If you create tension by pulling back on his leash or collar, he will just want to override the tension he feels, and you will reinforce his pulling.

I use three principles when teaching dogs not to pull me on the leash and to walk nicely with me. The principles of relaxed leash walking are very similar to the principles of establishing a good recall and allow me to have control of a dog without jerking or yanking.

1) Red light/Green light: Whenever you feel any tension on the leash, immediately stop moving. The quicker you are at this, the better it will work. You should stop for no longer than a second. Do not pull back on your dog's collar or leash. Start walking again the instant the leash relaxes. You or your dog can release tension on the leash. If he stops when you stop, take a step closer to him so that the leash relaxes and then start walking again. Don't expect him to back up. Likewise, if he slows down, stops, or turns his head even slightly and the tension on the leash relaxes, start walking again. Be quick; if you wait too long you will confuse him. He will eventually check in with you when he gets to the end of the leash by looking or glancing at you or in your direction. This is the first step in teaching him not to pull you.

Fig 45-46. Red light/Green light.
©2007 Margaret Crow

2) Mirror your dog by moving in the opposite direction: Mirroring your dog's movements will make him pay attention to you. You can turn it into a game. When he gets to you, reward him and keep moving. You can give him treats for looking at you, stopping with you, turning with you, following you, or coming to you. Move in different directions and encourage him to follow you the entire time. You cannot teach your dog to follow you on a leash if he is always ahead of you. You also don't want to trick him and jerk him so he that is afraid to move in a different direction than you. You want to teach your dog to follow you voluntarily. If he continues to head in a direction other than the one you chose and ignores your prompts to follow you, he will soon get to the end of the leash and you can implement "Red light/Green light." If he puts tension on the leash, stop moving. Don't pull him. Then encourage him to come to you, follow you, or run with you.

3) **Reward all movement in your direction and all attention that your dog gives you:** Behaviors you'll want to reinforce in your dog include attending to you on the leash, looking in your direction, not pulling on the leash, walking with you, turning with you, and looking at you. All these behaviors should be acknowledged, fussed over, and rewarded. Eventually he will see that he can't get to where he wants to go by pulling you and will then approach you. Reward him! If he stays by your side as you run or walk, praise him and give him treats. If he turns when you turn, reward him. Give him plenty of treats. Let him know when you are going to turn so that he can follow you and get rewarded.

Fig 47-50. Steps in relaxed leash walking.
©2007 Margaret Crow

Once your dog realizes that the goal is to walk with you on the leash without pulling, allow him to choose the direction you take on your walks. Let him choose where he wants to go and what he wants to see. If he starts to pull you, stop and change direction until he is focused and paying attention to you. Then go back in his original choice of direction. Let him go where he wants to go only if the leash is relaxed.

In addition to the three techniques above, you can teach your dog a "Let's go" cue that means you want to start moving again after you both have stopped for a moment. You may also want to teach him a sound that means that you want to change direction. Stand next to him. Say, "Let's go," and step forward beginning with the leg closest to him. Lure him to follow you. Give him treats as soon as he moves forward. To reward turning, make a noise as you change direction and give him treats when he turns to follow you. The best way to get him to turn with you is to secure his attention. Make a clicking or smoochy-kiss sound. When he looks at you, say, "This way," and turn. Reward him when he turns with you.

Finally, let your dog sniff. Dogs love to sniff on walks. People often become impatient and jerk on the leash to prevent their dogs from exploring interesting smells. If you try to prevent your dog from sniffing too much or become impatient and drag him, he will more than likely become obsessed with trying to catch any scent that he can. Let him sniff for a few moments. Then say, "Let's go," and reward him for beginning to walk with you. This will make him listen to you more often and be more receptive to your requests.

Unfortunately, we often teach dogs to pull us, and then we reinforce it. You can undo this habit, but it takes effort and practice. Getting the assistance of a positive trainer who uses similar approaches will help you to master these exercises.

Remember to practice good leash techniques and don't jerk on the leash!

Summary

- A Sof-touch leash has an elastic band near the end that helps prevent a sudden jerk on your dog's neck if you stop abruptly or suddenly change direction.

- A front-clip harness such as a Sense-ation Sensible or Easy Walk harness can make it easier walking a dog who pulls.

- A Gentle Leader or Halti can be helpful when managing aggressive dogs.

- Rewarding your dog for not pulling on the leash and for walking with you are the best ways to teach him to stop pulling.

- If your dog lunges on the leash, tense your muscles and keep your arms pinned close to your body.

- Don't jerk back on the leash if your dog pulls or lunges. Practice good leash control and body mechanics.

- A relaxed leash means that there is no tension on the leash where it attaches to your dog's collar or harness. You can keep him on a very short leash and still keep it relaxed around his neck.

- "Red light/Green light," mirroring your dog's movements, and rewarding him for paying attention to you, following you, and turning with you are good ways to teach him to stop pulling.

Teaching Your Dog to Stop

There is more than one way to teach your dog to stop while walking.

Begin walking with your dog by your side (either side is fine—just be consistent when beginning this exercise). Take a few steps with him, give a verbal signal for "Stop" (I say "Wait."), put the palm of your hand three to five inches in front of his nose, and then stop moving. Pause and reward him for stopping.

Dogs tune into noises and sounds that change frequency. A dog will pay more attention to you when you use words that change the frequency of your voice and when you add inflection. Also be sure to visually exaggerate the act of stopping.

When your dog regularly stops beside you when you stop, keep your hand in front of his nose but take a step past him. Then step back and reward him for stopping. Continue to do this until you can walk a few steps past him without him following you. Always return to him to give him a treat.

Teach your dog to discriminate between your verbal "Stop" signal and your hand signal. Walk with him by your side and give your verbal signal but do not put your hand in front of his nose right away. If he stops, give him a treat immediately. If he doesn't stop, put your hand in front of his nose and then stop.

Walk next to your dog toward a fence or other barrier. When you get to the barrier you both will have to stop. Give your verbal signal for "Stop" just before you actually do. Give him a treat for stopping immediately after he does so. Teaching him the exercise this way pairs your signal with the behavior of stopping. When you feel that he understands your signal, stand next to him, and begin to walk toward the barrier. Before you get to the barrier, give your verbal signal, and then stop. Reward him when he stops. Vary the locations in which you teach him to stop when he will regularly stop on cue.

While walking your dog on a leash, say your "Stop" signal just before he gets to the end of the leash. He will naturally stop when he gets to the end of the leash. Don't tug on or jerk the leash. Just stand still for a second. Repeat. Your dog will soon learn to stop before he gets to the end of the leash upon hearing your signal. When he does, give him a jackpot of treats! Be sure to give him your verbal cue before he gets to the end of the leash. Otherwise, he will not stop upon hearing your signal, but will wait until he gets to the end of the leash.

Practice giving your signal when your dog is closer to you. Give him treats for stopping before he gets to the end of the leash. When you are confident that your dog understands your signal, let go of the end of the leash when he walks in front of you; he should stop when he hears your signal. Don't forget to reward him profusely!

Chapter Seven

Pooch Etiquette—Positive Interactions at Dog Parks and Other Places Where Dogs Play

I love dog parks and animal-friendly hotels, bed-and-breakfasts, and beaches. You can help ensure that such places remain animal-friendly by learning proper doggy etiquette, which can prevent mishaps between your dog and other dogs. It is the owners' responsibility to ensure that their dogs behave appropriately at dog parks and other places where dogs are permitted.

Because new dogs entering a park can become overwhelmed by the number of dogs running over to greet them, do not keep your dog directly in front of the entryway to a park. You can teach him a good recall or to sit for treats whenever new dogs enter.

Stand up for dogs who are harassed by other dogs. Dogs who are continuously pestered or bullied by other dogs can be traumatized by the experience—especially if they are harassed by a group of dogs. Speak to the owners and let them know that they need to interrupt the interactions when dogs get harassed.

If your dog bullies a dog who wants to be left alone, redirect him to a more appropriate behavior, such as going for a walk or playing with a toy. Take him home if he will not stop harassing the other dog. The instant he begins to bully, subdue, dominate, mount, or pursue the other dog, give him a verbal warning. This warning will be meaningless to him at first. Try to redirect him to another behavior. If he bullies the other dog again after the warning, say your verbal warning again and give him a time-out or leave the park. Your timing is important. You must give your warning instantly when your dog behaves inappropriately. If he listens to your warning and stops bullying, praise him and allow him to continue playing.

Dogs who don't play often or who lack proper social skills need short and frequent positive encounters with other dogs. If you position dogs who lack social skills parallel to one another and focus their attention on activities other than direct social interaction, they will eventually become much more social and confident when together. Try taking your dog for a walk or a hike with another dog.

If your dog is shy, don't take him to the park when it is packed with dogs. Usually shy dogs like to meet new dogs one at a time or in very small groups. If your dog is shy and you want him to go to a park, use the park at off-hours or when you know there will be a few well-mannered dogs playing. Large groups are too scary for shy dogs. The best dogs for shy dogs to meet are other shy dogs.

Dog Fights

It is not hard to predict a dog fight—especially if you learn how to read canine body language. Changes in the intensity of a dog's growl may indicate that a fight is starting. When dogs play, however, there is no noticeable difference between the sound of a play growl and a real growl. You have to observe how the dogs are interacting with one another. If growling starts and intensifies without stopping, interrupt the play and let the dogs take a break or a time-out.

Any continuous repetitive behavior a dog exhibits, such as excessive pawing, humping, or mounting, may start a fight. The dog on the receiving end of these behaviors may become aggravated or frightened. A fight may also ensue if one dog continuously pursues another. Let dogs take a break from each other if any of these situations occur.

If two dogs are standing on their hind legs or making a lot of face-to-face contact without changing position, a fight may be looming. Distract the dogs from each other and positively interrupt the play. Remain calm and get the dogs focused on another activity.

Dogs raise and tap their paws on the ground and make play-bows when they play positively together. They will also regularly change positions and take turns being the offender and defender.

If a fight breaks out, take the following steps:

Make a very loud noise over the dogs' heads. This should interrupt the fight and give people enough time to secure each dog.

Pull the aggressor's tail or remove dogs from each other by pulling on their hips by the groin. Do not pull dogs by their legs, as this can seriously injure them.

Prevention and anticipation are the best ways to deal with fights. If a fight does occur, determine what caused it and then prevent those triggers from taking place. If the dogs were fighting over toys, don't bring toys to the dog park. If one dog simply dislikes the other, try to go to the park at times when the other dog is not around. Keep plenty of distance between dogs who do not like each other. This way dogs who dislike each other still have the opportunity to play with other dogs but do not have to interact with each other.

There is not much you can do after a fight has occurred. Reprimanding, punishing, or ostracizing your dog after he gets in a fight is useless. Not only will you fail to resolve any behavioral problems, you will exacerbate the situation by making him dislike the other dog even more. Instead, direct your dog to another activity, and remain calm. If you are angry at your dog, ignore him or take a short break from him. If he was attacked, don't baby him; act happy and positive and give him treats. If you become too upset he will also get upset. If you act positive and relaxed, he will recover quickly. Of course, if your dog was injured in any way, take him to the veterinarian immediately.

You can also deal with fights by counter-conditioning your dog to your grabbing his collar. Then, if he gets in a fight, his aggression can be redirected in a positive manner to the person who grabs his collar. By periodically touching and grabbing his collar or harness and giving him a treat, you can condition him to anticipate treats whenever his collar is grabbed. If a fight breaks out and you grab his collar, he will be more inclined to give you positive attention, as opposed to biting you or continuing to lunge at the other dog.

Use common sense when giving your dog treats in dog parks. Reward him for good behavior and, if he is shy, for socializing. If he guards you or is protective of his treats, do not give him treats when other dogs are close by.

Summary

- Keep your dog from hounding other dogs at the entryway to a park. Teach him a good recall or to sit for a treat when new dogs enter.

- Do not let your dog continuously pester a shy dog. Do not allow one dog to bully or harass another.

- If your dog is the bully, redirect him to more appropriate behaviors, such as going for a walk or playing with a toy. Take your dog home if he will not stop harassing another dog.

- Dogs who don't play frequently or who lack social skills need short and frequent positive encounters with other dogs.

- Large groups are too scary for most shy dogs. The best dogs for shy dogs to meet are other shy dogs. Walk shy dogs together to help get them acclimated to one another.

- If growling intensifies during play, give the dogs a time-out.

- Any continuous repetitive behavior a dog exhibits such as excessive pawing, humping, or mounting, may indicate that a fight is about to occur.

- A fight may break out if your dog constantly pursues a dog who is trying to get away.

- If two dogs remain standing on their hind legs while facing each other, positively interrupt the play and redirect them to other behaviors.

- When dogs play together, they will frequently position themselves next to or at a perpendicular angle to one another, and there will be a lot of paw-raises, play-bows, and changes in body positions.

- Understanding warning signs and interrupting play when it gets out of control are the best ways to prevent dog fights.

- To break up a dog fight, make a very loud noise over or near the dogs' heads, lift dogs by their hips, or hold on to the aggressor's tail. This should interrupt the dogs and give people enough time to separate them.

Chapter Eight

How to Choose a Trainer

It can be very difficult to find a good trainer. Whether the trainer or behaviorist is referred by a veterinarian, groomer, or another behaviorist or you find her in the phone book, you should ask a few questions before hiring. Years of experience are not as important as the methods and philosophy the trainer embraces.

Ask the trainer what equipment she uses or recommends for training a dog. A more positively oriented trainer will mention food rewards, play, treats, or a clicker. The trainer should use a flat nylon or fabric collar and harness or a martingale-style collar and a flat leash. A positively oriented trainer will not use nylon slip collars, choke chains (i.e., chain collars), pinch or prong collars, or shock collars.

Avoid trainers whose philosophies involve dominance or who talk about teaching dogs that you are the "alpha" or "boss," as well as trainers who label dogs stubborn or otherwise indicate that dog-training is based on reprimands and punishment.

Ask what a trainer does when dogs bark at each other in class. If she yells at, jerks, reprimands, or squirts water on dogs for barking, find another trainer.

A polished, skilled, positively oriented trainer will mention reinforcement, canine learning, rewards, ignoring unwanted behaviors, increasing the distance between dogs who are barking, and encouraging dogs to focus on you or to perform other behaviors if they are exhibiting behaviors that you don't like.

Avoid trainers who suggest a quick fix to a problem that you have barely explained. If you have a dog with a behavioral problem stemming from aggression, anxiety, or fear, a more skilled or positively oriented trainer will want to spend a few hours with you so that she can understand the problem. The trainer or specialist will ask you a lot of questions and may even ask you to fill out quite a bit of paperwork elaborating on problem behaviors and/or other concerns you may have about your dog. This information provides valuable insights so the trainer may better assess your dog's personality and how to best improve and resolve the situation for you and your dog.

Finally, watch how your dog responds to a trainer. If your dog is fearful, unusually hesitant, or seems to dislike the trainer, you may likely do better with a different trainer. Likewise, if the trainer ever criticizes or seems annoyed or frustrated by your dog or you feel in any way uncomfortable with how the trainer interacts with your dog, don't hesitate to find another trainer.

Your dog should feel safe and comfortable with his trainer. If your dog has any fear or aggression issues, a good trainer or behaviorist will not do anything to solicit, instigate, or encourage your dog's fearfulness or aggression. She will not intentionally frighten your dog or intensify his fears. If any trainer becomes in any way physically abusive, run—don't walk—away. Find a trainer who will treat your dog nicely.

A few organizations can be helpful when you're looking for a trainer. The Association of Pet Dog Trainers and the International Association of Animal Behavior Consultants are two reputable associations. The International Institute for Applied Companion Animal Behavior also has listings of trainers and behavior consultants who are dedicated to animal-friendly methods. However, membership in these associations does not guarantee that a trainer will abide by its philosophies. Even if a trainer is certified by or affiliated with a professional organization, be sure that she uses positive training techniques. Contact information for these two organizations is available in Appendix E.

Summary

- Years of experience are not as important as the methods and philosophies a trainer embraces.

- A more positively oriented trainer will mention reinforcement, canine learning, rewards, and to ignore unwanted behaviors. She will use food, play, and/or a clicker to teach dogs. A positively oriented trainer will not use nylon slip collars, choke chains (i.e., chain collars), pinch or prong collars, or shock collars. She will use a flat nylon or fabric collar and harness or a martingale-style collar and a flat leash.

- If you feel in any way uncomfortable with a trainer, find another one.

- Your dog should feel happy and comfortable around his trainer.

- Avoid trainers who bully or hit dogs or who adopt an "alpha" mentality with dogs, as well as trainers who squirt dogs with water, label dogs stubborn, or otherwise indicate that they use a training system based on punishment.

- If your dog has any fear or aggression issues, a good trainer or behaviorist will not do anything to solicit, instigate, or encourage his fearfulness or aggression. A good trainer will not intentionally frighten your dog.

- Look for trainers who belong to professional organizations, such as the International Association of Animal Behavior Consultants, the Association of Pet Dog Trainers, and the International Institute for Applied Companion Animal Behavior.

The Principles of This Book Summarized

- Use positive techniques to teach dogs.

- Always reward and acknowledge your dog for exhibiting desired behavior.

- Don't wait for your dog to exhibit a behavior that you don't like before you reinforce a behavior that you do.

- Pair anything that frightens your dog with experiences that he enjoys.

- Never expose your dog to stressors in a way that will upset him.

- Do not yank or jerk your dog on the leash—especially when he is around other dogs or people.

- Do not punish your dog for urinating or defecating in the house. Use proper housetraining techniques.

- Don't reprimand your dog for growling, lunging, or being upset.

- Desensitize and counter-condition your dog to things that make him anxious or frighten him.

- Teach your dog behaviors to perform in situations in which he feels unsure or uncomfortable.

- Get your dog a toy bin and encourage him to play with his toys.

- Learn good leash techniques.

- Hire a positive trainer to help you to teach your dog effectively.

- Always position your body at an angle to a dog. Stand or kneel next to or at a perpendicular angle to a dog.

- Pet your dog on his neck and chest and under his chin—not directly on top of his head.

- Do not stare down a dog. This does not establish dominance and will simply make the dog fearful of you.

- Pivot away from your dog and stop making eye contact if he gets too hyper and jumps on you. Give him attention when he is calm.

- Don't focus on your dog's unwanted behaviors. If you keep focusing on behaviors you dislike, you will spend less time reinforcing the behaviors you want.

- Dogs love to learn! Remember that training should be fun. Don't punish your dog; he will just become afraid of you.

Appendix A

Deaf Dogs

The best ways to teach a deaf dog are to use hand signals and positive reinforcement and to acclimate the dog to a routine.

Give your dog a vibrating/chime collar. You can teach him to pay attention to you when the collar vibrates, and the vibration can replace calling him by his name.

Teach your dog two hand signals: one for "good" and another for "great." The signal for "good" should mean one or a few treats or small rewards. The hand signal for "great" should mean a lot of treats or a highly desirable reward.

You will also need to teach your dog a visual release cue to let him know when you no longer have expectations of him.

Deaf dogs should only be allowed off leash in a secure or fenced-in area.

Deaf dogs can be startled by sudden touches or by being unexpectedly wakened. Desensitize and counter-condition your dog to being touched. Touch his shoulder and give him a treat, or put your hand in front of his nose to let your smell wake him. Give him a treat and/or lots of affection every time you wake him up or startle him.

Similarly, desensitize and counter-condition your dog to having his collar grabbed. Every time you touch or grab his collar something good should happen to him.

Some Web sites that address the needs of deaf dogs are listed in Appendix E.

Appendix B

Ari's Story (Sample Behavior Modification Protocol)

Statement by Nancy Bersani, Milton Animal League

"In June 2005, the Milton Animal Shelter received a call from another shelter regarding a puppy who was being returned for aggression and dominance. The family returning the puppy thought she should be euthanized.

Ari was a mixed breed puppy born on a small farm in March of that year. A woman driving by the farm saw a sign advertising puppies for sale. Ari was the only puppy in the litter that could be coaxed out from a hole underneath the shed where the puppies were living. The woman did not see the puppies' mother or father and was given no information about them. At the time, Ari was approximately 6 weeks old and infested with ticks. The woman's landlord did not allow pets, and after he discovered that Ari was living in the house the woman gave the puppy to the shelter.

The same day that Ari was surrendered to the shelter she was adopted by a family with two teenagers. After 10 days Ari was returned to the shelter again. The family called the shelter and said that they were bringing her back because of her aggressiveness. They felt that Ari should be put to sleep. Ari was now 4 months old. The shelter staff did not want to kill a 4-month-old puppy, so they convinced the family to bring Ari to our shelter (Milton Animal League is a no-kill shelter).

Ari was an active puppy whose reaction to any touch was to quickly put her mouth on you, leaving bite-marks and tearing clothing. The family stated that any physical correction (i.e., grabbing her collar and shaking it) resulted in a bite from Ari. If the person then shook the collar harder, Ari would respond by biting harder. When I took Ari outside to our fenced exercise pen she would run around the perimeter and then head straight toward me, jumping up on me (or anyone else within reach), grabbing clothes, skin, or hair in her teeth and leaving marks and drawing blood. Leashing her was a battle and initially took two people—one to distract her, and one to put on the leash. Ari would also chew everything in the shelter, including walls and doorways. I tried Bitter Apple spray, but she seemed to like it and licked it off!

A local behaviorist was working with Ari. She said that Ari was dominant. She used harsh corrections and punitive techniques. Ari's behavior became worse. We finally asked this woman to stop working with Ari. I instinctively felt that punishment was not the right approach. Because of Ari's behavior, I was the only person at the shelter who would work with her. A former MSPCA law enforcement officer began volunteering and took Ari for long hikes once a week. Ari looked forward to these outings, but she would always revert to biting and jumping on people, including the volunteer. No one thought she was adoptable.

We had recently heard about Alana Stevenson and I called her. She agreed to work with Ari and to set up a behavior modification plan for volunteers at the shelter to follow. Alana set up a positive, reward-based program for Ari that was to be followed by every volunteer who worked with her. Alana said that if people could not follow the recommended techniques then they should not be allowed to interact with Ari.

I started using the positive training methods Alana suggested. I began giving Ari treats for appropriate behavior and ignoring her for inappropriate behaviors. I walked Ari twice a day and threw toys for her in the exercise pen as long as she was behaving. I gave Ari treats for letting me touch parts of her body without biting me. Ari improved daily and could be worked with by anyone who followed Alana's recommendations. I continued with Ari and she improved so much that she rarely put her mouth on me. Since she was biting me hard enough to draw blood when she arrived at the shelter, this was a great improvement! People commented on Ari's improved behavior. In February 2006, after Ari was at the shelter for 8 months, a young couple adopted her. They followed our behavior modification recommendations. Ari has done remarkably well in her new home. People have complimented the couple on how well behaved Ari is.

Her new family is committed to continuing her training and only uses positive methods. Ari is great with everyone, including children. Ari is such a wonderful success story for our shelter!"

My Behavior Modification Plan

Nancy called me and told me that the Milton Animal League had been given a puppy from another shelter because the puppy was aggressive. The shelter volunteers thought that she was dominant. It had been recommended that she be euthanized; she was considered unadoptable. When she bit people, she punctured skin. I was told that a trainer had been working with her and considered her a very strong-willed and stubborn dog. I asked what kind of collar the trainer was using and I was told the trainer was relying on a choke collar. I agreed to see Ari and to set up a behavior modification plan for the shelter staff and other volunteers to follow. I highly doubted that a 4-month-old puppy would be dominant, and I had my suspicions as to what her problems were and how people were reinforcing them.

When I first saw Ari at the shelter, she used her mouth a lot when people touched her. Although I had been told that Ari was out of control when play-biting, it was clear to me that when Ari bit people she wasn't play-biting at all. Nor was she as aggressive or stubborn as her former family, the previous shelter, and the prior trainer had thought.

When I saw Ari interact with people it was clear to me that she did not understand how to respond to touch. She was sensitive to human body language and very reactive when people leaned over her or reached their hands toward her head or face. Based on the red marks, nicks, and scratches on Nancy's and other volunteers' arms, I could tell that Ari didn't have good bite-inhibition. This wasn't at all surprising, since she was only 6 weeks old when she was rescued. Ari's puppyhood lacked socialization, play with other puppies, proper chewing outlets, and any human consistency. Instead of taking the time to teach Ari how to play appropriately, her caretakers had reprimanded her for both playing and chewing. When Ari had experienced difficulty with being touched or handled, she had been reprimanded yet again. Since she had been passed around from shelter to shelter and from person to person, she had little understanding as to what it was that humans expected from her.

Being a social animal, Ari was desperate for attention. Ari wanted to interact with both people and dogs. However, since Ari was very intense and reactive with people, people were very punitive and reactive to her in return. This was a not a good start for a puppy.

Ari also jumped on people, pulled on the leash, and frantically barked and lunged at other dogs in the kennel. She walked by dogs who barked frenetically at her and so she growled and barked at them in return. All the dogs in the kennels were stressed.

I volunteered to work with Ari for a few hours and took her for a hike in the woods. When I interacted with Ari out of the shelter environment, I was able to observe her likes and dislikes. I quickly discovered that Ari loved swimming and was very bright and curious. I also saw that she definitely enjoyed having company. She seemed to like both men and women, which was good because it increased her chances of adoption. We passed by a small group of people and one came to pet Ari. I told the woman to stand next to Ari and to only pet her as I was treating Ari. Ari did very well. She did not jump on the woman or try to bite her. I allowed the interaction to continue for just a minute and then I redirected Ari to follow me and walk.

Ari bit whenever she wanted something. If we dawdled on the trail, she jumped and attacked my legs. She bit my hands when I held or restrained her. And when she bit, it really did hurt. When I brought Ari back to the shelter, I gave Nancy a behavior modification plan for volunteers to follow when working with Ari. My recommendations were as follows:

No one was to use punitive techniques or reprimands when working with Ari. She was not to be walked on a choke collar or be pushed down for jumping. She was not to be yelled at and no one was to grab her muzzle when she bit or tell her "No" when they disliked her behavior. These approaches had already failed to teach Ari how to behave and made interacting with people even more difficult for her.

I recommended that Ari be walked with a Sense-ation Sensible Harness. If she jumped on anyone that person was to pivot away from her, break eye contact, and ignore her. If Ari was relentless, the person was to remain motionless and wait it out or leave, but under no circumstances was anyone to interact with her or reprimand her for jumping. Anytime anyone touched her collar or any part of her body, she was to be given a treat; the yummier the treat, the better. When Ari seemed receptive to being touched and having her collar gently held, people could pet her and/or hold onto her collar for longer periods of time before giving her treats. I recommended that volunteers give Ari treats for any eye contact and attention she gave them when they walked her. Any time that she did not pull on the leash they were to praise her and reward her with play, food, and games.

Everyone was to stand or kneel parallel to or at a perpendicular angle to Ari. People were to always position their bodies at a slight angle to hers. No one was to approach her from the front, lean over her, or pet her directly on top of her head. If anyone wanted to pet Ari, this person was to be instructed to pet her under her chin and on her chest. People were only to interact with her when she was not biting or jumping.

I recommended that Ari be given treats whenever she walked by other dogs in the kennels. In addition, people could reward her for eye contact. The goal was for her to walk to her kennel—without barking at the other dogs—to get a special treat.

I also recommended that Ari be walked with other dogs. When she felt comfortable, she was to be allowed to play with other dogs in the exercise/play area of the shelter. It was crucial for her to have positive social interactions with other dogs. Finally, I advised that any follow-up training for Ari should come from a trainer who used only positive, reward-based methods.

A few weeks after Nancy implemented my recommendations for Ari's behavior modification, I was told that she had greatly improved. Because Nancy embraced humane, positive training, Ari was given a wonderful opportunity to have a nice life with a family who cares for her.

Every day I see many wonderful dogs whose potential could be realized if only people would take a step back and consider the dogs' needs. Unfortunately, our relationships with dogs are still often based on misunderstandings and ignorance. When people use compassionate training techniques, a beautiful partnership grows between humans and dogs. Our relationships with dogs can be based on love, respect, and friendship—not dominance, control, and obedience.

Appendix C

Undesirable Training Techniques

The following is excerpted from *Clinical Behavioral Medicine in Small Animals* by Dr. Karen Overall, V.M.D., Ph.D., 1997, and *Petiquette*, by Amy Shojai, 2005.

The **chin slap** is not a species-appropriate form of communication. Dogs have no clue what it means, so it will not correct a behavior and may prompt the dog to self-protect and bite back.

Damage caused by **the scruff shake** may parallel the cognitive damage caused by shaking a baby and results in increased activity levels and diminished attention. It makes training more difficult.

Chaining or tying dogs make them more reactive. A dog who can't escape can only respond to negative stimuli by fighting.

A review of **electronic training collars** indicated that all the dogs they were used on took longer to train than dogs taught without them and that the collars changed the dogs' play behavior (i.e., decreased the amount that they played).

The **alpha roll**, or forcing a dog onto his back, is used by trainers to establish dominance but makes fearful dogs more fearful and escalates aggression in aggressive dogs. Subordinate dogs willingly offer this behavior along with other calming gestures and signals. The alpha roll is based on misunderstanding and myth in how dogs relate to each other.

Hanging or "helicoptering" a dog by a choke chain and spinning him around by the leash causes brain damage and emotional changes, such as obsessive-compulsive disorders, increased generalized anxiety, and fearful behaviors.

Punishing a dog for what is not wanted, as opposed to teaching a dog what is desired and expected, is ineffective.

Appendix D

Food Treats and Edibles

Always begin training with the food reinforcer that your dog finds least desirable. If he will sit in the living room for kibble or just praise, don't give him your leftovers from dinner for doing so. He will not want to work for cookies and kibble if he gets his favorite food just for looking cute.

Use very small pieces of food as treats when training. The pieces should be small enough that your dog will want more when you are done training. You can feed your dog meals through training exercises or treat-dispensing toys or use kibble for beginning exercises. Use highly desirable treats when your dog is over-stimulated or distracted, when guests are over, or when he is outdoors, frightened, stressed, or anxious. If you haven't fed your dog a variety of foods, add treats to his diet one at a time. Don't give him too much all at once.

I tend to stick with less-processed food. Generally, whole food is better than the packaged variety. Avoid giving your dog treats that contain corn meal, corn syrup, or artificial colors and preservatives. Don't give him heavily processed or neon-colored treats.

I also tend to avoid processed liver treats and freeze-dried lamb, pork, and beef treats. These treats tend to be rich and can cause stomach and intestinal upset if given in large amounts. They also have very strong smells and are difficult for many people to work with.

Treats can be vegetables your dog likes. Fruit, brown rice, oat cereals, and peanut butter (ground, plain, and unsalted) can also be used for training. Your dog can lick peanut butter off a spoon as a reward. You can also use high-quality packaged dog food as treats during training. High-quality dog foods are available at independently owned pet-supply stores, health-food stores, and grooming shops. These foods usually do not contain "meat and bone meals," "by-products," corn, corn-meal, or artificial colors.

Most dogs like carob and molasses treats. I have a lot of success with them. They also smell really good. Crush hard or crunchy cookies into small pieces to make them last longer.

Most of what I buy is available online. Many of these products aren't available in regular pet-care stores. By all means, shop around! You may find treats your dog adores!

A Few Suggestions

- Best Buddy Bits Carob Flavor by Exclusively Pets
- Jump 'n' Sit Bits Carob Flavor by Three Dog Bakery
- Simon & Huey's Soft Treats Carob Molasses & Peanut Butter Molasses (www.SimonandHuey.com)
- Chocolicks Brownies and Cookies (www.chocolicktreats.com)
- Chocodrops
- Old Mother Hubbard's Vegg'n Biscuits
- Mr. Barky's Vegetarian Biscuits
- Blue Dog Bakery Peanut Butter Molasses Cookies
- Sam's Yams Veggie Rawhide and Big Boyz (www.frontporchpets.com)

Appendix E

Links and Resources

Please adopt an animal from a shelter or rescue league. There are far too many loving creatures who are in need of good homes. These animals are wonderful and are no more problematic than any of the animals you can buy from breeders. Some of these animals do need special help, but they can make great companions and will love every minute with you if you care for them humanely.

Animals in need of loving homes can also be found on www.petfinder.com. Remember to spay or neuter your companion dog, which will prevent and resolve many behavioral problems and will ensure that more unwanted puppies are not added to the already staggering numbers of homeless companion animals.

There are many wonderful books and Web sites available to help you learn about animal behavior. Here are just a few of my favorites:

Books

- *On Talking Terms With Dogs*, by Turid Rugaas
- *Feisty Fido*, by Dr. Patricia McConnell
- *I'll Be Home Soon*, by Dr. Patricia McConnell
- *Dogs Are From Neptune*, by Jean Donaldson
- *Don't Shoot the Dog*, by Karen Pryor
- *The Power of Positive Dog Training*, by Pat Miller
- *The Dog Whisperer*, by Paul Owens
- *Dog-Friendly Dog Training*, by Andrea Arden
- *Clinical Behavioral Medicine in Small Animals*, by Dr. Karen Overall
- *How to Behave So Your Dog Behaves*, by Dr. Sophia Yin
- *How to Right a Dog Gone Wrong*, by Pam Dennison
- *Aggression in Dogs*, by Brenda Aloff
- *Dogs Behaving Badly*, by Dr. Nicholas Dodman
- *How to Teach a New Dog Old Tricks*, by Dr. Ian Dunbar
- *Behavior Problems in Dogs*, by William E. Campbell
- *Bones Would Rain from the Sky*, by Suzanne Clothier

- *Canine Body Language: A photographic Guide Interpreting the Native Language of the Domestic Dog* by Brenda Aloff
- *Peaceable Kingdom*, by Dr. Jonathan Balcombe

Web Sites

www.doggonesafe.com
On dog bite prevention.

www.doggonecrazy.ca
Has a board game about canine communication signals and body language.

www.APDT.com
The Association of Pet Dog Trainers lists its members and can help you find a trainer in your area.

www.IAABC.org
The International Association of Animal Behavior Consultants is a professional organization that also lists avian and horse behavior specialists.

www.IIACAB.com
The International Institute for Applied Companion Animal Behavior is an educational resource for animal behavior professionals and endorses purely positive training methods and behavior modification techniques.

www.sitstay.com
Lists many good books on dog training and offers some great products.

www.petfinder.com
Search for animals available at rescue shelters across the U.S. Find animals currently available for adoption at local humane societies and animal shelters.

www.dogsdeservebetter.com

A nonprofit organization dedicated to rescuing and providing homes for chained dogs.

www.lcanimal.org

An organization dedicated to advocating the rights of animals and eliminating pet theft. Undercover footage of animal abuse at circuses, labs, slaughterhouses, and stockyards can be viewed on their site.

www.specialneedspets.com

Dedicated to handicapped pets. Also lists handicapped animals available for adoption.

www.handicappedpets.com

Offers products and services for handicapped, elderly, and disabled pets.

www.deafdogs.org

For owners of deaf dogs.

www.animalsentience.com

Devoted to the subject of animal conscious thought and feelings.

www.peta.org

People for the Ethical Treatment of Animals is an animal rights organization that focuses attention on the four areas in which the largest numbers of animals suffer: in factory farms, laboratories, the clothing trade, and the entertainment industry.